Praise for *Cats in the Belfry*

'The most enchanting cat book ever'

JILLY COOPER

'If you read *Cats in the Belfry* the first time round, be prepared to be enchanted all over again. If you haven't, then expect to laugh out loud, shed a few tears and be totally captivated by Doreen's stories of her playful and often naughty Siamese cats'

YOUR CAT MAGAZINE

A funny and poignant reflection of life with a Siamese, that is full of cheer'

THE GOOD BOOK GUIDE

Praise for *Cats in May*

'If you loved Doreen Tovey's *Cats in the Belfry* you won't want to miss the sequel, *Cats in May*... This witty and stylish tale will have animal lovers giggling to the very last page'

YOUR CAT MAGAZINE

Praise for *The New Boy*

'Delightful stories of Tovey's irrepressible Siamese cats'

PUBLISHING NEWS

DONKEY WORK

This edition published in 2009 by Summersdale Publishers Ltd.

First published by Elek Books Ltd in 1962

Summersdale Publishers Ltd
46 West Street
Chichester
West Sussex
PO19 1RP
UK

www.summersdale.com

Printed and bound in Great Britain

ISBN: 978-1-84024-719-0

DONKEY
WORK

DOREEN TOVEY

summersdale

Sadly, Doreen Tovey died in 2008, aged nearly ninety. She had thousands of fans of all nationalities and was surrounded by good friends and of course her two cats, Rama and Tiah, who were with her almost to the end. Over fifty years since her first book was published, she has delighted generations of owners of Siamese cats.

Also by Doreen Tovey:

Contents

ONE

Nettled

People staying in the district and hearing that we keep Siamese often stop at the cottage and ask to see them.

'Quiet spot you have here,' they comment, gazing idly round at the garden, the valley and the rolling West Country hills. That, say the more lynx-eyed of them a second or two later, spotting a pair of Seal Point ears protruding bulrush-fashion from a clump of grass on the far side of the lawn, must, from what they've heard of him, be Solomon. It is indeed. Solomon in ambush. In his favourite hide behind the air-vent of the septic tank, and a more embarrassing introduction than to say 'This is Solomon' – and then, when they enthuse about how beautiful he is and what *is* that interesting stone he's sitting behind, is it a Roman milestone, having to confess that that is the air-vent to our septic tank – it is difficult to imagine.

Flustered – some of them muttering doggedly that it looked like a Roman milestone anyway – they gaze around for inspiration. It is not long in coming. It arrives in the form of a pint-sized Blue Point queen within seconds of hearing people talking to Solomon. Belting down the path at top speed, dwindling to a coy dawdle when she nears the party – once, as the result of a springtime mousing expedition in the ditch, she appeared with her eyebrows starred with cow parsley flowers like the Primavera; we have often wondered how accidental that entry was... That, they say, greeting her arrival with delight, must be Sheba.

It is too, and a happy scene ensues with Sheba being cuddled, Solomon determinedly dodging his would-be cuddlers round the air-vent and everybody saying how they just love Siamese. Until sooner or later somebody spots Charles, my husband, in the vegetable garden or up on the hillside and asks, in a voice of dumbfounded amazement, 'What on earth's he doing with a *donkey*?'

She is our donkey, her name is Annabel, and we bought her because we had nettles. Two acres of them, growing waist-high round Charles' fruit trees with the village sages surveying them as gloomily as if they were mandrakes and saying 'twas a pity to ruin good trees like that, Charles unable to get at them because he didn't have time, and Sidney the handyman refusing to touch them because he said they was just the place for snakes. Sidney had a thing about snakes. He even advised us not to eat the watercress from the stream up the valley because, he said, it had little black snakes in it and his father knew a man what had dropped like a log after eating some for his tea one night. It was a moment of sombre triumph for Sidney when we asked how he knew it was the watercress. When they cut the poor bloke open, he said dramatically, there inside 'un was a little black snake...

Nothing short of a suit of armour would have got Sidney into the nettles. Charles toyed with the idea of a flame-thrower and discarded it because it might, he said, be difficult to keep it clear of the trees. (It might indeed; the last time Charles had used the blow-lamp he'd set fire to the garage door.) There was bracken growing between the nettles, too, and long ropes of bramble which, when Charles or I did venture up there with reaping hooks for a quick five-minutes' hack, caught us suddenly round the ankles and sent us leaping sky-high with thoughts of Sidney's snakes. All in all we were ripe as a couple of greengages for the day when, opening the Sunday newspapers, we found an article about donkeys.

Why more people didn't keep donkeys he couldn't imagine, enthused the writer. Neither could we when we read how in the old days farmers liked to run them with their cows (donkeys, it seemed, not only acted as herd leaders but cleared fields like magic of weeds which would spoil the milk); how they were no trouble to keep and cost nothing at all to feed if you had a piece of rough land – particularly, said the article, they liked nettles; how intelligent they were, and patient; and how, if you encouraged them and made a fuss of them, they would respond to you like a dog.

We looked at one another entranced. A little donkey eating down the nettles like a suction-pump. A little donkey cavorting between the apple trees, once it had cleared a cavorting space, like a character from Walt Disney. A little donkey – we smiled mistily at the thought – who would respond to us like a dog.

Charles and I liked dogs. We didn't have one because, whereas if we were away during the day we could leave a couple of Siamese cats companionably ripping up the stair-carpet or sleeping on the eiderdown, we couldn't leave a dog. Earthboxes we might have, but as Charles said, we weren't importing trees. We also didn't have one because, even if we had been around all day, the cats wouldn't have stood for it. A small black poodle called Prune, who lived down the lane and came flat as an ink-blot on his stomach under our gate in a way that had them spellbound with admiration, was permitted into the yard for biscuits. So was a corgi from up the hill, on account of his short legs at which they gazed with such interest that he invariably ended by tucking his tail self-consciously between them and scuttling crestfallenly away. But dogs in general – No. Certainly not in the house. Not unless we wanted fights and ambushes and cats leaving home in all directions, and we'd had enough of that the time we tried to adopt another Siamese kitten.

So there we were. Ripe, as I said, as a couple of plums. Telling ourselves that donkeys were different. That one could live out on the hillside without the cats being worried about its wanting to come indoors. They might, we envisaged, even think it was a little horse and like it. Solomon was particularly fond of horses... Imagining it following us across the hills like a dog – with Solomon and Sheba sitting one each side in panniers, said Charles enthusiastically, which I couldn't quite see coming off myself judging by the hell they created when we put them in their baskets ready for the cat kennels at holiday times, but there was no harm in hoping. We could, we told one another excitedly, hardly wait.

As a matter of fact we had to wait for six months. Donkeys, we found, weren't so easy to get. Particularly a baby donkey, which was what we'd decided on both from the point of view of bringing it up with the cats and because the first thing our neighbour Father Adams said when he heard we were getting one was that we'd have to watch the horse dealers. Do you soon as look, he said encouragingly, and we'd better watch their teeth. As we hadn't a clue as to how to watch either a donkey's teeth or a horse dealer's – and neither, when it came to the point, did Father Adams; only that it had been a maxim of his Dad's before him and his Dad, he said, had had his head screwed on when it came to horses – we decided a foal was safer. See it with its mother, we said (making sure that 'twas its mother, adjured Father Adams darkly, and not a little old dwarf donkey bunged up against a big 'un) and there we were.

There, to begin with, we nearly were indeed. Almost immediately Sidney heard of a donkey and foal in the very next village. The property, it appeared, of a lady who ran a guest house, liked getting up amateur theatricals for her visitors, and had, in a moment of over-enthusiasm, purchased a she-donkey eighteen months before to take part in a Christmas masque.

For, it seemed, one performance only. (Twice round the table-tennis room and that was that; never believe it, would us? said Sidney wonderingly.) After which the donkey had rested in the orchard until Spring, gone – her owner thinking she might be feeling lonely – to join the donkeys on the local beach for the summer; come back – to the consternation of her owner, who hadn't reckoned on her being as lonely as that – in foal. And now, said Sidney explicitly, there were two of 'em.

Not by the time we got there there weren't. Dolly pottering round the orchard on her ageing own had been one thing. Dolly with romance in the field behind the seaside gasworks in mind, and a jaunty little he-colt at her side, was quite another. You'd think they had wire-cutters the way they kept getting out, said their owner despairingly, and always it seemed to be at mealtimes, with visitors clattering their forks for service and somebody ringing up to say Dolly and Desmond had just passed by en route for the seaside and her having to hare down the road after them. In the end, she said – showing us with a sentimental sigh a photograph of two donkeys giving such old-fashioned looks at the camera that for a moment we almost wavered in our decision... Did it, enquired Charles, remind me of Anyone? I'll say it did. Solomon and Sheba to the life, but then I remembered we were only having one donkey and the apprehension passed. In the end she'd sold them, only the week before, to some people who lived near Manchester. People who liked donkeys, she said, and would keep the two of them together. Manchester, she added, brightening considerably as she thought of the advantages, was two hundred miles away.

It didn't occur to us that if donkeys could get out of a wired-in field how were we going to manage on rambling hillside land with gaps big enough for elephants in the hedges and not a gate to the place. It didn't occur to us that if we followed our plan of having a dear little she-foal (because, we imagined, she'd be more amenable and affectionate) sooner or later we'd either have a neurotic spinster donkey on our hands or have to let her have a dear little foal herself and keep two of them willy-nilly. We hadn't thought ahead as far as that. All we knew was that we wanted a donkey. Which was why the following weekend saw us down at the seaside, the lady at the guest house having given us the address of the place where she got hers, interviewing a donkey man.

TWO

Sleuthing on the Sands

We didn't get a little donkey from him. He didn't breed 'em, he said; only kept 'em for riding. When Charles mentioned Dolly having had a foal he said it was a surprise to him, too, Mate; the only stallion he had was over thirty-five and the fairies must have had a hand in it. He might, he said, spare us a mare at the end of the season like he had the lady at the guest house and we could hope the fairies had had a word with her, too... But that wasn't what we wanted.

We didn't get one from our next port of call either, though we did – against a background of small boys screaming to get on, small girls screaming to get off, and Charles trying to look dignified with a horse-drawn coach labelled the Deadwood Stage standing ostentatiously behind him – get quite a lot of information. That male donkeys are called jacks, for instance, and females are called jennies, and that what we thought were light little ponies cantering up and down the sands were in fact jennets. Crosses between horses and donkeys, said the man, and when we said weren't those mules he said that was when the father was a donkey. When the father was a horse, he said, you got a jennet.

Actually when we looked it up in the dictionary it said that what you got was a hinny, while a jennet was a small Spanish horse. That, said Charles, was genealogically very interesting. Donkey men were often of gypsy stock, lots of the English gypsies came originally from Spain – what was more likely than that they should call their donkey crosses after the small Spanish horse?

What struck me as even more genealogically interesting was that when I asked the man was it true that donkeys lived to be around forty, as it said in the article, he said sixty was more like it. He had a donkey at home, he said, that had belonged to his father, and his father had been dead sixty years so it showed how old the donkey was, didn't it? It did indeed, particularly as he himself couldn't have been a day over fifty. I puzzled over it for hours.

He didn't have any donkey foals either. He had a couple of jennies, he said helpfully, who'd be throwing 'em in the Spring and we could come back and have one then. The next two owners we enquired of also said their jennies would be throwing them in the Spring. Come April, it seemed, foals would be being thrown in all directions like apple blossom at a Spring wedding. What we wanted was one right then.

We didn't get it. The nettles grew and faded. The grapes ripened in the conservatory. We, having first waited till the grapes had ripened so that we could eat them, went on holiday to Provence so that we could eat some more. Up through the lavender fields to St. Paul de Vence where, in the last place on earth we expected it, right up there in the mountains, we met a Siamese cat. Sitting in a wood-carver's shop daring us to enter, and when we spoke to her and she was rude back her owner came rushing out to grab her and said not to mind Mignonne, she was a Siamoise. We, we assured her, understood. We had two Siamois. Aaah, she said, shaking her head sympathetically, at which point a small girl came round a corner hugging a black kitten. 'Mignette!' she said, holding it happily up for our approval. We looked from Mignette to Mignonne to the shopkeeper and raised our eyebrows. She raised hers too, and spread her hands in abnegation. What would we? she deplored. Mignonne, without waiting for the nice Siamois husband they had planned for her from a lady in Grasse, had gone out one night and been trumped. Mignonne had the final word about that. Surveying us loftily as she stalked across the shop to retrieve Mignette – it was Dark, she said over her shoulder.

We came back from the South of France – passing en route the swallows from our barn, according to Father Adams' grandson Timothy who will one day drive us mad with his efforts to be a naturalist, but we didn't recognise them. The cats came back from Halstock, on the one hand yelling that they were Home now for the Winter and we weren't to forget it and on the other recoiling from their plates with dramatic incredulity when we fed them, complaining that the Francises cooked better than that. Up the lane, to the doctor's horror, a builder started putting up a bungalow bang opposite his Queen Anne cottage – a situation complicated not only by the fact that the doctor didn't want it there but that the builder had promised some months previously to repair the doctor's chimneys and hadn't done it before starting on the bungalow. The doctor brought it up one day when he met the builder in the lane. Supposing they'd blown down the other night in the gale and come through the roof, he said reproachfully. Well they hadn't, had they? said the builder. His bark was worse than his bite, however. The next night he and one of his men went consolatorily up after they'd finished work on the bungalow and started on the chimneys. The only snag being that by that time it was nearly dark, they hadn't told the doctor they were going up (they couldn't, actually, because he and his wife were out) and when the doctor's wife came tripping back from her visiting, opened the garden gate, and saw figures prowling mysteriously round her chimney pot in the gathering gloom, she nearly fainted.

Winter was with us all right. The village cultural society started its Wednesday evening meetings and embarked on its usual round of setbacks. One night the lecturer forgot to come. Another night the electricity broke down. Another night it rained, the lady in whose house the meetings were held complained of footmarks on her brand-new Indian carpet and banished future meetings to the garden room.

Out there everybody froze and, when they had slides, the projector wouldn't work. An expert came to give a talk on Minoan architecture and nearly went mad because every time he said 'And now we pass on to the next Great Wonder' and tapped the table, only half a picture came on and that was upside down. The schoolmaster, re-connecting the projector, broke a piece out of the lampshade. The secretary offered to resign.

A few weeks later an expert came to give a talk on music, the lady of the house graciously allowed the society back into the lounge for the occasion on account of the piano, and there was another crisis. To protect the carpet she'd laid down a sea of thick brown horse blankets. That was reasonable enough, but when the expert tested us to see, as he laughingly put it, whether our musical intelligence was A or B; found it was somewhere around Z; pulled himself together saying Never Mind he'd give us a recital to pass the time – and found every time he put a pedal down it got caught up in horse blankets, he got pretty mad too.

It saw us pretty well through the winter. That; and the doctor, when the bungalow was halfway up, worrying about where its septic tank was going to be. His, because of the fall of the land, was piped under the road and ended in what would be the garden of the new bungalow and supposing they fractured his pipes, he said. By the time a man had come from the Council to sort that one out, not to mention the rest of the village making surreptitious surveys of the layout after dark and giving one another frights round corners... By that time it was Spring, and our thoughts turned once more to a donkey.

Almost at once we saw one advertised in *The Times*. A pigmy donkey at a ducal address on the other side of England – but that didn't matter, said Charles, as long as it was a foal and a good one. We could easily drive the couple of hundred miles to bring it back. It must have been a good one. Not only was it already sold when Charles rang up but it had gone for fifty guineas. I was there, hanging excitedly at his elbow, when Charles asked what it had fetched. When, without turning a hair at the reply, he enquired whether they had any more little foals for sale, and said in that case we'd watch the paper and perhaps in due course they would, I thought it must have been quite reasonable. When he put down the phone, looked at me with glazed eyes and said 'Fifty guineas' I felt quite queer. Charles felt so queer he didn't know whether he'd been talking to the duke or the butler. He didn't remember anything after the fifty guineas bit, he said. I felt so queer – though admittedly it transpired it was laryngitis – that I lost my voice immediately and it didn't come back for days.

We got one in the end, though. Not from our previous donkey-man. After all the optimism about baby donkeys popping up in all directions come April there was nothing doing there. Out of six owners their jennies had only thrown two foals between them, and both of those were jacks. We could, said one owner helpfully, board one of his in-foal donkeys if we liked, and then when the foal was born and weaned we could buy it off him and return the mother. We walked up the promenade in a positive dream of delight at that proposition, seeing a day-old donkey kicking its little heels among our buttercups, Mum standing bashfully by and the cats hilariously joining in the capers... until common-sense prevailed and we saw it as it more likely would be. Our sitting panic-stricken in the shed holding Mum's head, having to send for the Vet at midnight – paying for the privilege at that, said Charles, wilting as he visualised himself running up and down with hot water at two in the morning – and sure as eggs were eggs it would be a jack.

We rang a horse dealer who said Simple – about twelve pounds it would cost us, he said, and they were only the size of sheepdogs when they were small so he could bring one out in the car. He'd ring us when he got one, he said – and that was the last we voluntarily heard of him. Next time we rang him he said they were harder to get than we thought. Harder than he thought, too, apparently. We never heard from him again.

We rang a dealer seventy miles away who specialised in donkeys. A cute little jenny he had, he said. Eleven months old. We'd be lucky to get one younger than that – they weren't weaned till they were six months old and they were harder to get than we thought. Twenty pounds she was, he informed us, and a beautiful little off-white. Off we went, to find she was actually a sad-looking little off-grey. We wouldn't have minded that so much but she wasn't so very little either. She was almost as tall as another donkey which, he said, was a two and a half year-old riding jenny at twenty-five pounds. When we remarked on that he said they were nearly as tall at a year as they were at two and a half – 'twas their bodies that filled out, he said. It was also of course, if only we knew how to get at them, their teeth that grew. We did ask the man to open her mouth and he obligingly did, but we still didn't know what we were looking for, so we suppressed a shudder at the purposeful-looking set of teeth that he revealed, thanked him nicely, said we really did want a smaller one than that, and drove home.

We found Annabel the very next day. Just when Charles was saying we might as well buy a cultivator to get down the nettles – twenty pounds for a donkey plus transport was a bit much, he said, and now there were those teeth and supposing it bit the cats – I opened the newspaper and there she was. A demure-looking, shaggy little foal standing coyly by the side of her Mum at the one local resort we hadn't visited. Children were patting her head, parents were looking beamingly on. 'Everybody's Favourite' read the caption and Charles said he couldn't see her biting the cats.

We could, on the other hand, see her among our buttercups. We drove over straight away. It was raining and when we saw her for the first time in real life in the field beyond the beach she was standing knee-high in dock-leaves with a small green macintosh over her head. There was no doubt about her being young. Halfway through the interview she went and had a drink from Mum. He might, said her owner cautiously when we broached the subject, be prepared to sell her...

We examined her feet. One of the things we'd been told in our travels was that you had to be careful of soft spots in donkeys' hooves – spongy places which you can press in like sodden leather, caused in the case of imported donkeys by too much standing in the Irish peat bogs and for which, we were told, there is no remedy. We looked quite professional examining her feet, though there was really no need. She had been born in England, she was only ten months old, and her small polished hooves, the size of half-crowns, were as black and hard as ebony. We looked at her teeth – we still didn't know what we were looking for but they were apparently all there. We looked at her eyes. We couldn't see those at all. When we lifted the silky top-knot that covered her head like a floor-mop in reverse she had them modestly closed and all we could see was a sweep of long black eyelashes.

We bought her on the spot. Twenty pounds we paid without a murmur. Think, said her owner as he signed the receipt with a look of sorrow on his face, what he'd be losing by way of her attracting the children. Think, I said, struck by a fleeting attack of common sense on the way home, of how far that would have gone towards a cultivator. Think, said Charles, gazing happily at the sunset, of the fun we'd be having with a donkey.

THREE

She Doesn't Care for Carrots

The fun began the very next night when Annabel arrived by van, pattered demurely down the backboard, took one look round and immediately tried to patter up again. She didn't like us, she said from under her fringe. She was going back to Mum.

She looked smaller than ever standing there in the lane, with her shaggy brown coat, ears like a big toy rabbit and a set of sturdy little long-furred legs which, ending abruptly in those minute hooves, made her look as if she was wearing pantaloons. She was about the size of a sheepdog. She looked, said the Rector's wife who happened along just then and immediately went into ecstasies over her, as if you could have wheeled her along on her dear little feet like a toy on castors.

She might have looked like that, but there was good solid donkey under that winsome exterior. She wouldn't be led, and when Charles and the donkey-man tried to push her she planted her hooves firmly in the lane, settled her rear practisedly against their hands, and pushed back. They looked, said the Rector's wife, watching rapturously from the garden gate, like a group by Rodin. They did indeed. The Boulder-pushers in granite.

People who believe you can move a donkey by dangling a carrot in front of its nose are, I can assure them, quite wrong. I didn't just dangle it. On account of her possibly not being able to see it because of her fringe, which was particularly bouffant that evening, I put it actually in her mouth, let her take a bite, and started walking enticingly backwards with it towards the gate. Only I moved. The Rodin group stayed exactly as it was. Nothing happened at all except for a couple of village men who cycled past with ostentatiously rigid backs and said to one another as they turned the bend 'Didst thee see that?' Annabel didn't care for carrots.

When, by dint of practically carrying her, we finally got her into the paddock next to the cottage where she was to stay till we put her out on the hillside, Annabel didn't care for that either.

She was going now, she said, determinedly following the donkey-man to the gate where, with a last sad fondle of her ears and instructions that that was car oil on her bottom through rubbing against the van and we could wash it off with Omo when we had a fine day, he left her. She was going now, she reminded him when he started up the engine. She couldn't believe he was leaving her behind. She stood with her ears pointed incredulously after him as he drove off up the hill and when we lifted her fringe and bent down to speak to her there was no doubt about it at all. Annabel was crying.

We did everything we could to comfort her. We fetched the cats. Far from consoling her they spent the rest of the evening on the garden wall, alternately craning their necks at her over the brambles like a pair of Indian scouts and beating it for the cottage like a pair of Indian arrows when she brayed.

We fed her with bread and a piece got stuck. We'd have called the vet within her first hour with us if it hadn't been that while we were deliberating how we were going to break it to him that we *had* a donkey – he was already, as we knew, inclined to lean his head against the wall and groan when we phoned him about the cats – Annabel got it up herself, dropping a soggy piece of crust into my hand with a thankful gasp.

Eventually, having provided her with water that she wouldn't drink and straw that she wouldn't lie down on, we went to bed. Not to sleep. Our idea of animals at night was the cats curled comfortably in the spare room armchair with a hot water bottle, or the squirrel we used to have who slept in our wardrobe; not a forlorn little donkey in a field crying for its mother. What, we wondered – while Charles kept interrupting our train of thought with the suggestion that perhaps we should put her in the conservatory for the night so she'd feel closer to us, and I kept saying she'd break the glass – had we let ourselves in for?

One thing we'd let ourselves in for was the loudest voice in Christendom shouting unremittingly for Mum. Annabel didn't, to correct another fallacy about donkeys, say hee-haw. She went AAAAAAW – HOO – AAAAAAW – HOO – AAAAAAW – HOO – FRRRMPH at approximately half-hour intervals. Long enough to allow for listening for a reply from Mum in between. Long enough for the neighbours to drop off into a fitful sleep from which they must be leaping galvanised in their beds by the next AAAAAAW – HOO – FRRRMPH as if Gabriel was sounding the last trump. And in a voice which, if they didn't know there was a baby donkey in the valley, they might well mistake for a jungle elephant's.

We shuddered when she did shout. We worried when it was time for the next bray and she didn't. At one time instead of a bray a sort of gulping noise came through the night. What, enquired Charles anxiously, did it sound like to me? A strangled gasp I said as we bounded out of bed. Annabel was tethered on the advice of the donkey-man who said if we didn't, until we got the place wired she'd be on her knees and through the gaps in the hedge bottoms as soon as our backs were turned and we imagined her with her rope wrapped round a hawthorn bush choking herself to death.

We were saved from tearing up the lane in our dressing-gowns by the fact that Charles, who was only half awake, insisted on putting on his socks as well and while he was fastening his suspenders Annabel let out such a fanfare – probably at hearing him move, for she seemed to have very good hearing – that it was obvious there was nothing wrong with her. Charles took off his socks, rolled back into bed and started snoring with exhaustion. Annabel, hearing him from the paddock, sent forth an answering call which if it once more roused the neighbourhood at least roused Charles as well and stopped him snoring. From the cats' room came a succession of bumps and padding noises as they kept getting up to look out of the window. And so the night wore on.

We'd had nights like that before, of course. The night we acquired the squirrel. The night we acquired our first Siamese. The time we tried to add Samson the kitten to the household and Solomon and Sheba stayed up all night threatening to take him apart. Life always seemed more liveable the next morning and apart from the fact that when Charles opened the spare-room door this particular next morning the cats, instead of tumbling down the stairs with enthusiastic demands to be let out, filed silently past him into our room and got into bed with me – Tired through being up all night, said Solomon, subsiding heavily across my neck; got a Headache, said Sheba, vanishing crossly beneath the bedclothes – things weren't too bad at all.

Annabel was still there for one thing, with her fringe cocked raptly at us over the mowing grass. The sun was shining. Solomon, emboldened, no doubt, by the fact that he hadn't been murdered in his bed while he slept after all, came spying cautiously round a grass clump at her while we gave her breakfast and, when she looked at him, purred. By the evening, our confidence soaring like a temperature chart, we were taking her for a walk.

Like a temperature chart it pretty soon went down again. Annabel, plodding demurely up the lane with Charles and me beaming proudly on either side and Solomon trailing us interestedly in the rear, did the length of a sixpenny donkey ride – and that, she decided, was that. Turning determinedly for home she began, in approved donkey return-ride style, to trot. Never having given donkey-rides herself, of course, but just having accompanied Mum, she didn't realise she was supposed to stop at that. Within seconds the trot had become a gallop, the gallop – with Annabel kicking her heels light-heartedly behind her as she went – had become a charge, and I, holding frantically to the end of her rope and shouting to Charles for help, was going down the lane behind her like a kite.

Charles held her rope the next night, while Solomon and I followed behind. We needed firmness, he said, if we were going to train her like a sheepdog and sure enough when we got to the sixpenny mark and once more she stopped and we, putting our shoulders to her rump, were firm practically to the point where our arms dropped off, it worked. Once past that point and she ambled up the lane like a lark. Like a lark, too – to use Charles' description of her as he walked proudly at her side – she turned when directed at the forest gate and began to amble back. And like a lark, the moment she rounded the corner and could see the long straight stretch of lane ahead, she began to fly. Much faster than the previous night. Solomon and I were delayed only for a matter of seconds by his stopping to look down a mousehole en route and by the time we rounded the corner there was no sign of Charles or Annabel at all. Only a cloud of dust settling silently in the distance.

They were in the paddock when we got back – Annabel eating dandelions and Charles leaning breathlessly on the gate. Annabel, as she'd done the previous night with me, had frightened the daylights out of him by pretending to be set for a top-speed tour of the village and then zooming into her paddock at the last moment. Annabel, we were to discover in the days that followed, had that kind of sense of humour.

The next night, to avoid coming back each time as if we were practising for the Grand National, we took her on a circular tour. Up the valley. Over the stream. It took us twenty minutes to cross that on account of Mum having apparently warned her to keep away from water, and the only way we did it was by eventually going over ourselves, leaving her behind and commenting loudly that we didn't want her. Whereupon, with a snort to us that she was Coming and another one to the stream to be careful otherwise she'd deal with it – over she came. Stopping immediately to eat a plantain to show her independence, but nevertheless she was across.

After that we met a man with a dog and Annabel, towing Charles and me like a couple of tugboats, chased it. After that – while we explained that she liked dogs and was only playing and the man indignantly said it looked like it, didn't it, butting a poor little spaniel in the backside like that – she ate a foxglove.

At least, said Charles, as with aching arms and long past the time we'd expected to be back we turned at last on to the track leading down to the cottage, we wouldn't have to run back this time. Annabel didn't know the track from Adam.

Undoubtedly she didn't. Either she could smell her way, however, or donkeys have an amazing sense of location, for hardly were the words out of his mouth when she began to gallop. Down the hill in the gathering dusk like a sheepdog-sized toboggan. Mane flying, legs flying, Charles and I running frantically behind her. Past the cottage, with the cats watching round-eyed from the hall window. In at the paddock – when, Charles told everybody afterwards with pride, she might so easily have passed it in the twilight. Annabel knew her home now coming from any direction. Where, she demanded with a snort as Charles and I clung mopping our brows at the gate, was her supper?

FOUR

Annabel and Friends

We learned quite a lot about donkeys in those first few days, and Annabel learned things too. To drink water, for instance, which was quite a feat for previously she'd only had Mum's milk. When I offered her bread and milk she sniffed and said it was Cow. When, after a whole day when she didn't drink anything and we wondered once more whether we should call the Vet, she suddenly got the hang of it and we found her with her nose blissfully in the bowl sucking water, our joy really knew no bounds.

Solomon, who was with us when we made the discovery, knew no bounds either. Gazing incredulously from the shrinking water to her fur-lined ears – Solomon, when he drank, lapped with the sound of high seas smacking on the pier at Brighton and he couldn't understand why Annabel did it so quietly – he was quite unprepared for the bit at the end when she lifted her head with an appreciative slurp. Solomon, about six inquisitive inches from her nose when it happened, gave one big leap and was gone.

Solomon was doing a lot of leaping just then. Sheba, pursuing her usual course when she wasn't too sure of a thing, pretended Annabel didn't exist. She could be found imperturbably thinking on the garden wall, talking to Charles from the coal house roof or, if it was absolutely necessary to pass the paddock, marching down the middle of the lane with eyes fixed straight ahead as if following a Cats' Guild banner. Solomon, drawn by his insatiable curiosity as to a lodestar, could be found approaching the paddock from all directions on his stomach like a Mohawk, peering at her through grass clumps and – on occasions which nearly turned our hair white – sitting in her bed.

After her first all-night shouting session Annabel had taken to her bed – which was straw laid in a small stone shed under an elder tree – like a duck to water and Solomon, to use Sheba's usual description of him, was being silly. It was evident from the jaunty way he sat there, yelling invitingly at us from the straw. It was evident from the way, when we went to get him out, he went dashing round the paddock with his ears flat saying he wasn't coming. It was evident from the way – when Annabel spotted him herself and went after him in a style that reminded us, as we rushed sweating to his aid, of a charge by a North American bison – he came shooting out shouting That was a Near Thing and the next moment went dashing back to sit in it again.

Wasn't it delightful to see them getting on like that? Asked our dear old friend Miss Wellington, who had appointed herself our mentor in animal-keeping from the time we had our first Siamese and was now supervising our guardianship of Annabel. As 'like that' constituted Solomon at that moment running like the clappers for the gate and Annabel going as hard as her hooves would travel after him we couldn't say. All we could do was hope.

Annabel by this time, of course, should have been out of temptation's way as far as Solomon was concerned – up on the hillside eating nettles round the fruit trees. She wasn't because, the way things have of happening with us, the night she arrived the man who brought her took one look round at the orchard and said he'd thought we meant *grown* fruit trees, not tiddling little things like that. Eat 'em down like sugar-sticks she would, he said, and we'd better build her an enclosure if she was to go in there. One with chicken-wire sides she couldn't get her head through, and move it round as she ate down the nettles.

That, of course, took some planning. And while we were planning it – going round with poles and tape-measures saying this bit was too steep for her to stand on and that bit was too much in shadow and she must have her quota of sun – Timothy turned up with his Curfew shall not ring Tonight expression on his face and informed us that she'd die if we put her in there.

He had, it seemed, looked it up in one of his nature books and discovered that bracken was bad for horses. It wasn't surprising because Timothy was always finding something dire in his nature books and arriving to announce it to us in the style of Hamlet. That hemlock was confusable with cow parsley, for instance, or that if Solomon ate Deadly Nightshade he'd die. Solomon wasn't in the least likely to eat Deadly Nightshade, but by the time Timothy had analysed the possible results of Solomon eating Deadly Nightshade berries, Solomon eating Deadly Nightshade flowers, Solomon eating Deadly Nightshade leaves, and finally Solomon merely sniffing Deadly Nightshade plants in passing, it gave me the willies to the extent where I went round pulling up Deadly Nightshade plants for miles.

It was the same about the bracken. When we looked it up ourselves it was to discover that it was when it was sharp and brittle that bracken was dangerous, not when it was young and tender. The question was, when did it become sharp and brittle? Not yet, one would have thought – in May, with the fern-fronds pale as peas and coolness in their depths. But Charles snapped some experimental stalks and said they seemed sharpish to him, I snapped a few myself and confessed they seemed sharpish to me... The upshot was that Annabel, bought to eat down the orchard, now looked like reposing in the paddock for months, till we had time to cut out the bracken by hand.

Meanwhile she'd begun to draw her audience. First, the morning after her arrival, there was the neighbour who drooped tiredly up the lane and said so that was what it was – his wife had been waking him up all night saying she could hear sea-lions. Next there were some workmen en route for a cottage they were renovating up the lane, going by while Charles was in the paddock with her and calling matily over the gate 'Got yerself a friend, then!' Next there was the owner of the corgi, gazing peacefully around him while his dog ate some grass and jumping practically out of his shooting breeches when Annabel greeted him from behind the hedge. And eventually there was the whole village.

They came to see Annabel even more than they'd come to see the cats. Perhaps, said Charles nostalgically, she reminded them of their childhood. Seen from the cottage garden, with her tufted ears, puff-ball fringe and white snub door-knocker of a nose gazing steadfastly at us over the wall, she reminded me more of the Abominable Snowman, but she certainly had what it took.

They commented on her size – the littlest they had ever seen, they said, and would she stay like that? They commented on her coat. Never – said the ones who asked us about it – had they seen a long-haired donkey before, while the ones who didn't ask us stood at her gate in droves and assured one another that she was a Shetland pony. They brought her carrots and peppermints and she began to develop tastes. Annabel, reported a neighbour on the phone one night, was certainly getting choosy. She'd given her some ginger-cake the first day she'd met her and she'd eaten it like a dream. Her husband had taken some things down this morning and she'd spat out the ginger cake, eaten the iced one, butted Donald with her head when he didn't have any more and then retrieved the ginger cake.

That wasn't the only way she was developing. Annabel, born and bred in an open field, slept in her house at night now as to the manner born. Trustfully on her side in the straw, with a preliminary period before she went to sleep when she lay in the doorway with her head out and her hooves crossed like a dog, peacefully contemplating the night. Gosh, she was intelligent! said Charles, who went up every night to look at her over the fence and came back to report the fact of her lying down as if she'd passed the Eleven Plus.

Annabel, like his other girl-friend, Sheba, only had to wiggle an ear-tip for Charles to think she was one of the world's wonders – but there was no doubt that she was intelligent.

When she'd emptied her water-bowl, for instance – a big, two-handled, white-enamelled pan holding a couple of bucketfuls – she didn't leave it just standing there waiting to be found by accident. She turned it upside down. Not only could we see it immediately from the cottage, but usually she didn't have to wait even that long. Annabel's bowl bottoms-up by the door of her house, and Annabel standing demurely by the side of it like a flower girl with big ears selling violets, had people leaping the fence like Commandos. Our rain-water barrel went down as if an elephant was draining it with people coming in saying we didn't mind, did we, but the donkey was thirsty, washing the bowl under the tap to get the bits out, and bearing it lovingly back to her again.

She took care of herself in other ways, too. When the donkey-man told us donkeys liked to roll, for instance, and we ought to provide her with an ash-patch, we said Oh yes and dismissed it. It was summer, we didn't have any ashes – and Annabel, we decided, would much sooner have nice fresh grass to roll on when she got used to it.

Annabel wouldn't. Annabel wanted ashes. As we didn't give them to her, first of all she scraped an ant-hill flat to the ground in her paddock with her hoof and rolled in that – with the obvious follow-up from Solomon that the moment her back was turned he rushed in and rolled as well and we knocked a few more years off our lives leaping in to snatch him out – and then, on about the fourth of our nightly promenades up the lane, she discovered the cement. A good half-sack of it, spilled in the lane in front of the cottage that was being renovated.

Then, and every night afterwards until it rained and at long last turned the stuff solid, Annabel not only returned from her walk at a gallop, she set out at one as well. Up the lane to the cottage, where we stood helpless in a cloud of cement dust holding her rope while she rolled. Praying nobody would see us, because our tale was how easily we managed her. Praying, too, that when she eventually stopped rolling we could get her home unseen because by this time, proud though she was of the result, she looked more like a dirty old goatskin rug than she did a civilised donkey. Praying quite in vain, of course. People came round the corner like pins to a magnet while Annabel lay there rolling or fanning cement over her rear with her tail. They passed up the lane, it seemed, in *hordes* when she was on her return journey, with her coat puffing cement dust like a pair of bellows at every step. What with that and Solomon's habit, when she was back in her paddock, of sitting bolt up-right on a stone outside the gate – Guarding his dear little Friend, said Miss Wellington, though if we knew anything of Fatso he was more likely to be shouting Sixpence for a Donkey-ride or playing trainer at a circus... what with one thing and another she was getting quite well known.

Notorious would perhaps be a better description. We were coming now to a week which we'd planned, with the cats safely under lock and key at Halstock, to spend resting from our labours down in Devon. We'd had Annabel in spite of these arrangements because we thought if we left it for a fortnight someone else might snap her up. Some friend or other, we reasoned, would undoubtedly have her in their orchard while we were away – or if not we could board her at a local riding school.

Some friend or other might have done if it weren't for the fact that most of them had young orchards like ourselves, two of them withdrew after hearing Annabel do her AAAAAAW-HOO-FRRRMPH, in case, they said, the neighbours complained, and Annabel nipped the remaining one on the shin. Only in fun, it could hardly have hurt at all, said Charles, and if the Molleys didn't understand donkeys better than that he'd rather they didn't have her.

He needn't have worried. They didn't intend to – which left the riding school as our last resort. We got round to deciding we'd rather leave her there anyway – with people who *understood* animals, we said, and we could, guess what a fuss they'd make of Annabel – grooming her, training her, taking her out with the riding procession like a little regimental mascot... and Annabel gummed that one up by frightening the horses.

She'd already done it once, it seemed, while we were away in town. The first we knew of it was the following Saturday when we were in the paddock with Annabel; her fringe was looking particularly fetching, the riding school was clopping up the lane towards us, and Charles said this was just the time to ask.

Before I could, the voice of the riding mistress was heard through the trees. 'Coat's too long. Wants clipping,' she commented as she approached. 'Isn't she hot?' she said to me as she passed. 'Mind the donkey!' she called commandingly rearwards in the same breath. At which Annabel bounced joyously forward to greet them, the horses at the end of the procession stood on their hind legs with fright, a shrimp-sized rider sitting adroitly on the top end of a whacking great chestnut said she'd done that on Thursday and Wufus had been tewwibly fwightened, and as the cavalcade moved on up the lane – 'Horses don't like donkeys' came the final verdict of the riding mistress.

Cows don't like them either, apparently, until they are used to them. Annabel spent her holiday eventually on the local farm where the farmer, who fell for the fringe on sight, first of all said she could go in with the cows and the bull and then – in case, he said on second thoughts, the bull should chase her – put her in a little half-field to herself, with a ladder closing the gap into the big main field where the cattle were.

You can guess what happened there. No sooner was his back turned than Annabel, filled with joy at seeing a field full of friends all ready for her to play with, got on her knees, crawled under the ladder, and began to chase the herd.

Nobody remembers noticing the bull. All they saw was a tide of cows surging across the field followed at a gallop by Annabel; the Rector's wife coming unwittingly along the lane; the moment of impasse when the parties met at the farmyard entrance – the Rector's wife staring aghast at the leading cow, which in its alarm had its front feet over the gate, and the leading cow, with its escape blocked, staring equally aghast back at her – and finally the moment of relief when, with the farmer leading Annabel firmly away by the scruff, everybody could relax again.

After that, and a further scare when they found her halfway through the hedge one afternoon – looking, she said, for buttercups – they put her on a tether. After that one might have thought they'd be glad to see the back of her.

There was, we decided as we led her home on our return – unrepentant, kicking her heels blithely as she went, threatening to butt the farm-dog under the milk-chum stand as she passed – no accounting for tastes. They said she could come again.

FIVE

Miss Wellington is Worried

Things settled down quite quietly for a while after that. As quietly as things could settle, that is, with a donkey with a voice like Annabel's.

She rarely cried at night now. She slept peacefully in her house beneath the elder tree until our alarm woke her up at half-past six. It meant, of course, all the neighbours waking up at half-past six as well because the moment she heard it, thinking we were greeting her from our bed, Annabel immediately shouted back at us from hers. But nobody minded that. Either they went to sleep again, thankful that she'd let them stay that long, or else, if they had to go to town themselves, it was a useful aid to getting up.

They didn't even mind the odd occasions when she did shout at night. She did it now only when she was disturbed and it imparted either the interesting knowledge that we'd come home in the early hours and Annabel was greeting us – whereupon they would mention the next day that they'd heard her kicking up at two this morning and we had naturally to admit where we'd been and what we'd been up to – or else it meant that somebody else had come home late and we could all, in the time-honoured way of villages, having a rattling good time working out who that must have been instead.

She shouted during the day, of course, but only by way of talking. To us, when she saw us in the garden. To people (anticipatorily) who came to pet and feed her and to people (reprovingly) who jolly well didn't.

We learned to tell the difference between her calls in no time. A semi-silent AAW-HOO-AAAAW, performed almost to herself with an excited intake of breath and much running up and down the fence, meant we were coming, perhaps to take her out. A louder, more sustained AAW-HOO-AAAAW, like a rusty saw being worked at top speed, meant the Rector was coming down the hill with an apple, or his wife with a biscuit, or somebody else Annabel recognised with a piece of cake.

A raucous, trumpeted AAAW-HOO-AAAAW – ear-splitting and ending in a snorted FRRRRMPH! – meant that Annabel was indignant. Charles, perhaps, had gone into the garage without bringing her a peppermint, or the baker had gone past the paddock without stopping to cluck at her, or worst of all and producing the most reproachful FRRRRMPH of the lot – the riding school had come into view. Not passing her gate as in the old days but crossing at a cautious distance over the side of the hill, with the riding mistress circling the group like a sheep-herder.

Annabel stood watching hopefully from her paddock when they appeared, quite unconscious of the fact that she was being avoided. Down Here She Was, she trumpeted as soon as she spotted them. Down HERE, she shouted as they plodded heedlessly onwards. They were going the WRONG WAY, she yelled at them after an unbelieving pause. ROTTEN LOT OF SNOBS JUST BECAUSE THEY WERE HORSES, she bawled when it became obvious that they weren't going to take any notice. FRRRRMPH! she sniffed disgustedly as she turned away and began to eat ash-leaves to show how little she cared,

She shouted at cars when they stopped and cars when they took off. She bawled pleasantries at the builders' men till she got them bringing her cake and apples too. One day an extra-large delivery van arrived with the bath for the cottage that was being modernised, backed up the lane on the advice of a villager who said they'd never get out again if they didn't, and got the top hooked on the branch of an elm tree outside Annabel's paddock. Hung up like a hat on a hall-stand said Father Adams, who'd watched them with interest from his gate. And while the driver and his mate were debating whether to borrow a saw, turn the van round and try again or leave the bath at the roadside, Annabel stuck her head through the hedge behind them, enquired at point-blank range whether they happened to have any sandwiches they didn't want and thick old townies, said Father Adams, slapping his knees with joy at the recollection, went up as if they'd taken Kruschens.

That was all very well, but Annabel's voice carried. Up the hill and round the bend till it reached Miss Wellington, busily working in her cottage garden. And Miss Wellington, hearing that voice like everyone else for a good two miles around, echoing up the valley in strong competition with the cuckoo, immediately began to worry.

It was fatal when she did that. She worried once about Father Adams' pig being on its own and for weeks she spent an hour each evening doing her knitting by its pigsty. Standing bolt upright by the pigsty gate, which produced a much more urgent effect than if she'd done it sitting down, and saying it was company for Daisy. Which was more than it was for he, said Father Adams, who when he saw her nipped smartly out of the back gate and up to the Rose and Crown.

She'd worried another time about what she thought was a neighbour's cat. A big fat black one which she kept seeing sitting soulfully on the neighbour's doorstep and which, being Miss Wellington, she kept opening the door and letting in again, announcing loudly for the neighbour's benefit that it was draughty on the doorstep and she was sure its Mummy wouldn't mind.

Actually its Mummy minded very much. She was new to the village. She had, though Miss Wellington didn't know it, two black cats, both exactly alike. Right then she was trying to keep them at the back of the house because she had someone staying with her who was allergic to cats while the cats, typically enough, were marching indignantly round to the front door saying they wanted to go in *that* way. What with Miss Wellington popping them in at the front and their owners putting them out again at the back they were going round like Red Indians doing a war-dance by the time the new people discovered who was responsible, and they weren't half mad with Miss Wellington when they did.

In our case Miss Wellington decided that Annabel was shouting because she was lonely, and when we said she wasn't, she was only talking, she said we didn't Understand. In order to convince us that we didn't understand she started inviting friends to tea who apparently did, and bringing them down to see us. Nearly every day when we were home a little group could be seen advancing down the hill around half-past four. All ladies. All of somewhat indeterminate age. All dressed like Miss Wellington in macintoshes and – as it was summer – straw hats that had been rained on and gone rather bumpy-looking in the process. And all nature-lovers to the last eye-tooth, in evidence of which they darted about the lane like dragonflies as they came, picking little bunches of flowers.

At this time of day we were usually having tea ourselves on the lawn and Charles, if he spotted them first, was not above slipping out of his deck-chair on all fours and making for the garage. What most often happened, however, was that there was a coy little cry of 'ANNN-abell!' from Miss Wellington, Charles swore soundly into his teacup, and when we looked up there they were, standing in a group on the corner, gazing enchantedly across the garden at our donkey.

Annabel from that angle was a particularly enchanting sight. All you could see of her was her head. The wall hid the rest of her from view and the Alice in Wonderland effect of her rabbit ears, enormous puffball fringe and inquisitive white nose framed in the tall May grass filled her visitors with delight.

They swept up the lane to pet her like a swarm of bees. When we for politeness' sake left our tea and went up to join them, there they were having their flowers eaten and their coat-hems pulled, one of the party was by that time generally clasping her jaw and assuring her companions that she could hardly feel it, and Miss Wellington was looking worried.

Not about the jaw. That was the result of somebody bending down to whisper affectionately in Annabel's ear and Annabel whose idea it was of being affectionate back, docking them soundly under the chin with her nose. That Miss Wellington, who never remembered to warn people that Annabel did it dismissed with an absent-minded smile. Lucille, she would inform us anxiously as we approached – or Violet, or Agatha, or whoever she considered the most impressive of this particular batch – was afraid that Annabel was lonely.

When they marched back up the hill again Miss Wellington, despite the weight of her supporters, was still looking worried. Annabel, we informed her at least three times a week, could not go and live with the riding school for company. The horses didn't like her. Annabel, we said, could *not* wander loose in our garden. We wouldn't have any plants. Annabel, we explained, could *not* have another donkey to talk to because we only wanted one and anyway she talked to us. Annabel, we assured her, was perfectly happy as she was.

Annabel certainly should have been. She had her own house with a tarpaulin roof to keep out the rain, she had her own paddock with a private ant-hill on which to roll, and by this time – despite Miss Wellington's conviction – she was acquiring a wide circle of friends.

There was the marsh-tit whom she allowed to perch on her back and, while she stood demurely in the sunshine, take beakfuls of her hair for its nest. There was the blackbird who pottered unconcernedly round her feet for breadcrumbs while Annabel, as we crept quietly closer to watch, looked down with tilted ears and a benign little droop of her lips to see him do it. There was Prune the poodle with whom Annabel had struck up the same sort of friendship she had with Solomon consisting of watching him with invitingly lowered ears while he got in through her fence and then chasing him round the paddock like a Derby runner. Just to confound all the rules, there was also an Alsatian and a horse called Major.

Annabel, according to the man we bought her from, didn't like Alsatians. Little dogs she could butt with her nose were acceptable, he said. And, he had no doubt, Siamese cats. But not Alsatians, one of which had chased her as a baby and she'd been scared of them ever since... On the understanding that horses didn't like donkeys, it gave us quite a turn one morning when we glanced out of the window to see a great grey hunter towering over the fence, looking patronisingly down at Annabel in just the way we'd seen her looking at the blackbird. On the understanding that Annabel didn't like Alsatians, it gave us even more of a turn when we took another look and there, leaping wildly at her ears and apparently about to seize her by the throat at any moment, was an Alsatian the size of a wolf. We went up the garden like greyhounds. At times like this I realised the probability of Charles's forecast that with the sort of animals we kept we'd still be running when we were ninety.

She hoped we didn't mind, said the owner of the animals, who when we got there was leaning patiently against a tree – but Major, her horse, was mad about our donkey and wouldn't pass the paddock till he'd seen it, and Misha, her Alsatian, insisted on having a game. While we watched with trembling knees they *had* a game. Misha put his head under one strand of wire and drank from Annabel's water bowl while Annabel leaned over another and apparently bit his tail. Misha rushed into the paddock, leapt playfully at Annabel's ears, and Annabel butted him with her head. Side by side, apparently doing their best to knock one another flat, they cantered round the field a couple of times at least before, with a last nip at her ear and a bark which presumably meant he'd see her again tomorrow, Misha bounded up to join his owner. What, said Charles as the riding party moved off up the lane while Annabel watched them from the gate with the air of a small girl seeing guests off from her birthday party – would Miss Wellington have thought of *that* as company for Annabel?

What would she have thought, if it came to that, of the morning three of the riding school children turned up on foot and asked if they could take Annabel for a walk. It was a fine opportunity for exercise for her, and with reservations we agreed. They were only, we stipulated, to take her up the valley where she couldn't run away. If she did get loose, said Charles, at which they raised professional eyebrows at one another and sighed politely inaudible sighs, they must come back and tell us immediately. They shouldn't, I advised them, walk too close to her head in case she butted. Or too close to her heels, put in Charles, in case she frisked and kicked them by accident.

With that, and final instructions that she wouldn't cross the stream except when we were with her and to watch out if she rolled because although she was small she was heavy, they set out. One each side, one behind and Annabel plodding demurely away in the middle, like a string of miniature Canterbury pilgrims.

It was two hours before we saw them again. Two hours during which we kept looking anxiously up the lane assuring ourselves that of course they were all right and we mustn't fuss. Two hours in which we kept imagining the children butted over banks or rolled on by a rioting donkey, Annabel with a broken leg or running lost among the hills, and the lot – when time went on and neither she nor they showed up even independently – down one of the local pot-holes.

When suddenly they were at the back gate, having done a complete circuit of the valley and come down the hill behind us. She hadn't, they informed us as they hitched her expertly to the gatepost, tried to roll or gallop or butt them once, and she'd walked absolutely for miles. She'd gone over the stream without a pause, they said – they couldn't think why we thought she wouldn't. Could they take her out again?

Annabel was doing very well for friends indeed, and it was a pity Miss Wellington couldn't know. Miss Wellington was on holiday, however. Staying with a friend near Clovelly. Sending us cards with donkeys on them, invariably in groups of two or more, with a message that had the postman positively mesmerised. SOME DAY, enquired the cards in large capital letters – THIS?

SIX

The Donkey Owners

They supposed, people sometimes commented in suitably saddened tones, that the cats were settling down now and that was why we'd bought a donkey.

Those were the people who didn't own a Siamese themselves; who took at its face-value the sight of Solomon sitting soberly on the field wall watching Annabel and of Sheba, who'd at last got round to acknowledging that there were such things as donkeys and we had one of them in the paddock, sitting equally soberly beside him. Bless their dear little hearts, they would sigh. Pity they got older, wasn't it?

Those two weren't getting any older. The fact that Solomon's normally orchid-spotted whiskers were temporarily snow-white and contrasted oddly against his seal-black face, and that Sheba had gone white too, all round her mouth and nose so that it looked as if she'd been dipped in face-powder, had nothing to do with age. Way back before we'd had Annabel they'd been ill, and the whiteness was part of the aftermath. They were six now and fighting fit again, and as fiendishly bad as ever. Even their illness had resulted from one of their escapades. One of Solomon's in point of fact, though Sheba encouraged him in it.

Solomon had decided he was a tom. He'd decided it some time previously, when a real stray ginger tom appeared on the scene and, to show there was a man around at last, started to spray about the valley. Solomon, not to be outdone, immediately started to spray back. An action not unknown in a jealous neuter, particularly in a Siamese, but which we had so far not experienced. He not only sprayed wherever the ginger tom had been... On our Rockery Wall, he would announce, examining it with dark suspicion as he passed and immediately backing up to it to effect his own contribution... On our Garage Door, he would add a second or two later while Sheba watched with admiration and said fancy his being able to do that... On our Loganberries, he informed us on one occasion and without more ado bang went the loganberry crop for the season before our very eyes... but he sniffed.

Round the garden, under the gate, up the lane – he followed the trail, being Solomon, with the sniff of a Hound of the Baskervilles and a spray with the force of a Flit gun. We tried to stop him, knowing the risk. We sprayed the lane ourselves with disinfectant till people stopped and sympathetically asked us whether our drains had gone wrong. It was no use. It was a hot dry summer, we couldn't disinfect the entire countryside though goodness knows we tried, Solomon followed the trail with gusto and the next thing we knew he had a germ and was lying, a sad small shadow in a blanket, with a temperature and a swollen tongue. He couldn't eat, he couldn't drink, he dribbled and he was very ill.

Our only consolation in the anxious days of nursing him was that Sheba was unlikely to get it. From the moment she walked wide-eyed into the room on the first day of his illness, sniffed cautiously at him over the top of his blanket and backed speedily away saying he was Catching, we weren't nearly so much worried about Sheba picking it up as unnerved by the precautions she took to see that she didn't.

Passing the invalid's couch in an exaggerated circle, for instance, presumably in case he leaned out and breathed on her. Leaping defensively on to the table when from time to time, not knowing quite what to do with himself, Solomon got feebly down and tottered across the room. Let them sleep together, said the Vet, because if it was infectious she was incubating it anyway and meanwhile she might comfort him. But when we put them in the spare room at night, laying Solomon tenderly on his favourite corner of the settee and inviting her to cuddle up to him, Sheba took up quarantine stations in the other corner, with a good big ridge of blanket between herself and the germy one, and refused to comfort anybody.

Five weeks after Solomon's outbreak, with Solomon himself convalescing nicely, the Vet declaring five weeks' incubation was unheard of and she couldn't possibly have it and Sheba looking sorrowfully at him saying she was afraid she did, she began to dribble too.

At that stage we had the further complication of Solomon, now he was on his feet again and it wasn't him the Vet was coming to give injections to, taking such an interest in medical affairs we were scared stiff he'd reinfect himself. Where Sheba had kept away from him, for instance, the moment he came into the room he strolled up and took deep diagnostic sniffs at her stomach. When we put cream round her mouth in an effort to get her to eat and she listlessly left it there he bounded forward, saying it was a pity to waste good stuff like that, and ate it off himself. When I gave her water with a teaspoon, trickling it gently into her mouth as she lay frailly in Charles's arms, he nipped up behind us and had a good long drink from the bowl in case it contained something special. And when we shut him out through one of the sitting-room doors to keep him away from the germs it was only a question of seconds before Solomon, having streaked like a black-faced hare through the kitchen, round the cottage and through the porch, was coming through the other door, agog with excitement to see what we were doing to her now.

He didn't reinfect himself, in due course we reached the happy day when two fit Siamese cats – one big, black and important-looking; one small, blue and extremely self-possessed – sat side by side in the cottage porch. We hoped, we informed Solomon as he sat looking interestedly round the garden, that this would be a lesson to him and we'd have no more of this business of being a tom. It was, of course, like water off a Siamese's back. The next stage in Solomon's campaign of being a tom was that he had to have a girl-friend.

Solomon didn't like girls. There was a blue one down the lane, a black and white one up the hill, Father Adams' Siamese Mimi if he felt like company of his own superior kind... Solomon never had liked girls. Silly, prissy things, he said. When he saw them he chased them as he did the toms, with the exception of Mimi who was apt to chase him back. For the demonstration of the next step in being a tom he chose, of all people, Sheba.

Both of them were neutered and it couldn't do any harm but it was embarrassing, to say the least, to be walking down the lane and several times en route have Solomon suddenly spring on Sheba, grab her by the neck, and start howling through a mouthful of fur to Look what He was Doing. Particularly since Sheba, after the first couple of times when she kicked him in the stomach and fled, decided to co-operate. There they posed, Sheba flat on her stomach uttering coy feminine cries with her nose in the dust, Solomon holding her manfully by the scruff and daring the ginger tom to get his Woman. Been seeing too much television, commented Sidney. Dear little friendies playing together, beamed Miss Wellington when they did it outside her gate. Absolutely disgraceful, said somebody one day who fortunately we didn't know.

Disgraceful or not, they went on doing it. Never in the house or garden, only when we were coming back from walks, and only when we were far enough ahead for them to pose before we could stop them.

It meant – for the information of psychiatrists who may see in this some evidence of sad frustration – absolutely nothing. In their minds it was part of the fun of the walk, like shinning up the fire-warning notice when we came to the forestry gate and drinking from muddy puddles, and it was forgotten the moment they got home. It was also typical of Siamese, a fitting answer to the suggestion that now they were six they were settling down, and it carried them inevitably on to the time when Solomon caught up with the ginger tom again and got another germ.

This time they fought in the garden shed and the tom gashed Solomon on the cheek. That, judging from the tufts of ginger fur we found scattered in the shed next day, with Solomon going gloatingly in to look at them every time he passed, was nothing to what Solomon had done to the tom. But it was enough. A fortnight later Solomon started sitting by the fire looking sorry for himself. The next day his tell-tale third eyelids came up, with Solomon peering woefully over the tops of them looking like Chu Chin Chow. Once more Solomon was sick.

It was fortunate, the Vet assured us, that, spectacular as it looked, the illness wasn't dangerous and lots of other cats around had had it, because Solomon said he was dying. Freezing, he said, huddling up to the fire for warmth. Couldn't See, he wailed, raising his sad veiled eyes to us for sympathy. When he ate it was even sadder. His appetite was unimpaired, but when he bent his head the effort set the tears running down his cheeks and into his food, and poor old Fatso ate them willy-nilly with his rabbit. On and off he had stomach-ache as well which was why, of course, his eyelids were up; as a sign of intestinal disturbance. Poisoned! he would yell, leaping violently to his feet whenever a pang struck him and frightening us into a sweat.

A fortnight later Sheba appeared one evening with her third eyelids up, announcing that she was poisoned as well, and we started all over again. Six weeks the infection took from start to finish. Eight in all for the pair of them, allowing for the fact that Sheba developed it a fortnight later. At the end of that time, save for the fact that they were considerably thinner and their whiskers had whitened under the strain they were as fit as ever while we, after what we'd been through, were a good deal nearer Colney Hatch. A few weeks later we had Annabel. The fact that the cats could be seen so often after that sitting soberly on her paddock wall had, as may now be appreciated, nothing to do with age but was a sign that they were waiting for us to arrive. So that they could pursue their latest interest, of being Donkey Owners.

Being donkey owners meant patrolling our side of the fence, while we fed her, with superior looks on their faces. Our side of the fence because it showed they belonged to the boss class, could rub possessively round our legs, stroll out to the lane when they liked, and walk importantly back to the cottage with us when we'd finished. Annabel's side of the fence was reserved for Solomon's racing sorties – when he tore madly into the lion's den to show how brave he was, sat in her bed and had to be hauled out again. Annabel's side of the fence, as far as Sheba was concerned, was reserved for strolling nonchalantly through when we were on hand, sitting down with her back to Annabel, and looking around.

Nice in here, she would announce, her back a study in sublime, pale blue indifference. Better before we had a donkey of course. *She* remembered it then. *She* remembered it Always. In here now, she would comment, ambling innocently through the grass towards Annabel's sleeping house while Annabel raised her head to look after her, we used to have... At which Annabel would stop eating and chase her and Sheba would dash through Annabel's bed, leap smartly on to the wall and shout for Charles to rescue her. Not that she needed rescuing. It was just a tradition of having to be saved by Charles at every opportunity that Sheba had kept up since kittenhood. Left to herself, as we discovered on the odd occasions when Charles was in sandals and had to fetch his gumboots from the cottage before wading through the nettles to get her out, Sheba would pass the time of waiting rolling blissfully in the slack of Annabel's tarpaulin roof, a scant two inches above Annabel's vengeful ears, as nonchalantly as you liked.

SEVEN

As Sure as a Siamese Cat

Time passes swiftly in the country. Sheba's nose began to turn blue again. Solomon's whiskers, to our great relief, started to grow out spotted. Up the hill the bungalow was finished; the people, who were very nice, were living in it; the only snag, by way of one of those situations that are typical of village life, was that the doctor was now more involved about his septic tank than ever.

Initially he'd worried in case the builder damaged it. After that he'd worried because it was now officially inside the new people's boundary and how, he said, was he going to get in to examine it? In order to be obliging the new people had accordingly fenced off the land under which the tank lay into a sort of little lane so that he could examine it whenever he liked. On reference to the maps it had in any case been discovered that the doctor's predecessor had, twenty years before, unwittingly put the tank under a right of way to a disused quarry, and nobody in their senses would have a right of way through their garden in a village for a moment longer than they could help. And now the doctor was worried about that.

Tradesmen's vans, seeing a convenient turning lane suddenly opened up to them, started to reverse in it. Twice the doctor had gone out at night and found a courting couple parked in a car in it. Supposing they went through the concrete cover, he demanded, and was not one whit comforted by Father Adams' observation that he didn't suppose they'd like it very much either.

The doctor said it ought to be barricaded to protect his tank. The village said he couldn't block a right of way, he couldn't, 'twas against the law, and watched hopefully from its windows to see if he did. The doctor put a couple of boulders pillar-wise in the entrance and, confident on the one hand that the tank was safe while people could still walk the right of way if they wanted to, was now worrying on the other in case a car backed into the boulders, as everybody predicted, and claimed on him for damage. Made life interestin', din' it? commented Sidney.

Down in the valley life was equally interesting. Annabel was growing up. She was, which we very much regretted, beginning to lose her coat. She'd rubbed a good two inches off her fringe on the paddock wire and now we could see her eyes. Beautiful eyes they were. Dark, demure, slanted with a doe-eyed softness that was quite enchanting. Except when she was feeling stubborn about something and showed the whites of them at us.

Charles said she'd probably been doing that under cover of her fringe ever since we'd had her. Maybe she had. All I know is that Annabel rolling her eyes at me incognito was one thing. Annabel rolling her eyes so I could see them, with what remained of her fringe sticking rakishly up on top like the comb of a rebellious cockatoo, was very definitely another. When we went for walks for the next few weeks, even though it was summer and people stared, I wore a duffle coat, gum boots and gardening gloves, kept a weather eye open when she was behind me, and felt a whole lot safer.

Meanwhile Annabel was beginning to evolve at the other end, too. By dint of industriously rubbing her rear on a convenient ash tree she'd worn down her coat until from her woolly brown pantaloons there were beginning to emerge the smooth grey rump and slender legs of a young she-donkey. A little odd-looking when one viewed her from behind. Rather on the lines of a statue appearing inch by inch from a block of somewhat woolly stone. Far more graceful than we would have expected – she was, we told each other with pride, while yet we regretted the passing of her baby Shetland look, going to be a very attractive filly donkey. And at the same time strangely touching.

Touching in that when we walked behind her and watched those sturdy young legs trudging along with the typical forward-leaning stance of the donkey, as though already she was pulling some heavy load, we could see all the donkeys through the ages in her small but powerful gait. Plodding the deserts and the mountain tracks. Young and strong and eager when they started; weary, beaten and defeated when they were old. The donkey, which has been –and in some countries still is – the worst-treated of all animals by man.

That, we said at such poignant moments, hastening to fondle her ears and rub her nose while Annabel stood demurely between us contriving to look Worse Treated than Anybody by reason of the fact that we now put a halter on her when she went out, would never happen to our little donkey. Our little donkey was going to stay with us for ever.

You bet she was. Our little donkey, in a few short weeks, had us where she wanted us as surely as if she was a Siamese cat. She wouldn't even wear her halter the way it was meant to go, which was round her nose and behind her ears. When we put it on like that she stood stock still, closed her eyes, and refused to budge. She didn't, we were given to understand from her coy but firm expression, *like* things on her nose.

We thought it rather sweet the first time, when we lifted her fringe to reason with her and there underneath was Annabel with her eyes shut. We didn't think it nearly so sweet when we tried it after she lost her fringe and she still closed her eyes the moment we put the halter on. Now her objection was obvious to the world and while we were trying to reason with her invariably somebody would come along and say, Look at that donkey with its eyes shut, and somebody else would say, Poor little thing, fancy treating it like that, and then they'd glare at us and we would sigh and take the halter off and put it on again the way which Annabel approved. Round her neck in a big loose loop, as she'd worn her rope when she came to us. Making her look – seeing that we'd bought her a show halter which was wide and white and noticeable – as if she was to be shot at dawn. And so we would set forth. Annabel trudging

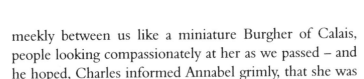

meekly between us like a miniature Burgher of Calais, people looking compassionately at her as we passed – and he hoped, Charles informed Annabel grimly, that she was happy.

She was. She was even happier when, unable to stand being looked at as if we were executioners any longer, we decided the time had come to try her without a halter at all.

Annabel following us freely round the countryside was like a dream. True it was offset by intermittent nightmares when we went near traffic roads or through the village and Annabel had to go on her rope for safety. Then – by way of rebellion even at that slight restriction now that for most of the time she ran free – she drooped and wilted on the end of it in a way that turned us hot and cold with embarrassment. Usually outside people's cottages, where we reached a state of complete impasse because the only form of persuasion that worked with Annabel in circumstances like these was to smack her bottom.

If we smacked it by hand a cloud of cement dust rose from her coat, our hands went numb, and Annabel, her nose sunk dreamily in a clump of toadflax on somebody's wall, informed us via the stolid set of her rump that she hadn't felt a thing. If we smacked it with the halter-end Annabel moved at once, but with such a downcast droop of her head and a tucking-in of her tail – in case, we understood, we Beat Her Again – that we hated ourselves on the spot.

Whichever we did we could depend on somebody appearing immediately in a doorway with a look that indicated one finger more on that dear little donkey and they'd call the police. And there, while Annabel *Frrrmphed* friendlily at them between mouthfuls, lowered her eyes so they could see her eyelashes and generally indicated that this was the first time we'd let her stop for days, we waited. Sometimes for what seemed like days too, until Annabel, with a final sad farewell *Frrmph* that doubtless meant See them in the Salt Mines if she lasted that long, ambled slowly on down the road. We'd read about Stevenson using a pin on Modestine. We couldn't, under any circumstances, have done it ourselves. But, as Charles remarked many a time and oft as we stood there waiting for our own particular donkey to develop a glimmer of conscience and get a move on, he knew how Stevenson felt.

Twenty yards round the corner, away from the traffic roads, away from cottages and the need to impress their inhabitants and minus her rope, Annabel was a different donkey altogether. She still lingered to eat when she came to a particularly tasty patch, but with the air now of an independent deer stopping to graze, not a captive grabbing a last few mouthfuls en route for the hulks. And there was no need to cajole her to follow us. We only had to walk on round the bend and, with a drumming of hooves and the flash of a familiar pair of ears, Annabel was with us. Only for a second, mind you. A kick of a heel in our direction as she went to show that she wasn't really following us – she happened to be going this way herself and we'd better jump for the ditch Or Else – and Annabel was past us. Zooming round the bend ahead, whence she would either appear a second or so later coming like an express train in the other direction or else – if it was dusk and she was wondering whether we meant to go much further – peering cautiously back at us round the corner.

Annabel didn't like the dusk. She was frightened of the shadows and refused point blank to pass the cement patch in the dark because it shone whitely at her and she thought it was a ghost. Annabel wasn't as tough as she pretended in many ways. She knew our usual route through the forest – up the valley, across the stream, over the moor-top and down the hill behind the cottage – like the back of her hoof. She galloped that, in daylight, practically non-stop – backwards and forwards as we walked; leaping the stream like a steeplechaser now, not wading it with tremulous fear; and all this in a size so small it was like seeing a rocking-horse come to life.

We watched her, scarcely able to believe it. That a donkey could move like this, as fast and graceful as a colt. That she had this desire to stay with us even when she was free and full of spirit. And that if we did stop en route, to sit by the stream in the valley or admire the view across the river from the top, fast though she might be galloping when we halted, Annabel would stop too, and draw quietly nearer in the background. Close enough to keep an eye on us. Far enough, according to her lights, for us not to know she was doing it. And there, till we moved, she would wait. Our donkey of two months' standing.

On unfamiliar ground her determination to stay with us was even more noticeable. We would perhaps come up a track with a minor one leading from it and, calling Annabel, who in strange surroundings was apt to stop and gawk around her with the air of a tourist taking in the Grand Canyon, we would turn off along the side one. Annabel, wresting her interest a second or two later from an intriguing rustle in the undergrowth or a speculation as to whether it was worth going the other way to see what it was like up there, would look round, see that the main path was empty, and start galloping. Past the turning we'd taken, on till she came to the next bend and then, when she found we weren't around it, her hoofbeats would stop.

Sometimes she would gallop back. Sometimes she apparently crept back on tiptoe, because the first we knew of her being in the vicinity was a pair of ears poked antennaewise round a nearby bush. For quite a second or two until, having satisfied herself that she'd found us but we couldn't see her, could we? back she would come with a snort and a gallop, to pass us and start grazing a few feet ahead.

There were snags, of course, to letting her run free. One was that we didn't imagine this business of her creeping around on tiptoe. Sometimes she caught us up at a gallop. Other times, when the sense of humour took her, she came up behind us so quietly that the first I knew of it was a yell from Charles as she nipped him in the rear, I jumped yards with fright – and there, when we looked round, was Annabel right behind us, head demurely bent, eyelashes fetchingly lowered, and with an unmistakable wobble to her underlip which meant she was being funny. Guess who did that? she would enquire, looking coyly at us with her big brown eyes.

That was why – though I agreed with Charles indubitably that she was joking and it was only a pinch and it showed how much she liked us – that I usually walked ahead of him. That was why for quite a while, as an extra precaution, I always went out in a duffle coat. If Charles liked having his pants bitten by a donkey by way of affection I most certainly didn't. And that was why, on these long, free walks with her, we couldn't take the cats.

She might have nipped one of them on the tail – only in fun, but the result would have been two cats up the nearest pine tree and ourselves ringing up the fire brigade. She might have kicked them as she galloped. Again quite by accident. Annabel's kicks, light-hearted as a breeze; were never calculated to land. We'd long noticed that when she passed us in a wide track her kick was wide, too – exuberant, outflung as an arabesque and apparently missing us by a mere hair's breadth – but that when she passed us on a narrow path her kick was narrow to match. A mere slight sideways tipping of a hoof as she passed, and the surest proof she could give that we were friends and she was only playing.

But Solomon, when she galloped, got excited and galloped too. He and Annabel were doing Agincourt, he would roar, pelting along at her heels, his ears streamlined with excitement, filled with his old ambition to be a horse. So, just in case she kicked Henry the Fifth by accident, not knowing he was there, we entered on a new department of the daily routine whereby we took them for walks separately. Usually – for the sake of variety – in opposite directions. With the result that people doing circular tours in the neighbourhood would quite often meet us going up the valley accompanied, to their interest, by a pair of Siamese cats – up trees like monkeys, complaining that the lane was Wet or pretending to be courting – and then, coming back an hour or so later in the opposite direction, they'd meet us going along with a donkey.

They stared like mad the second time. They eyed us from beneath their eyebrows as if we were not quite all there – which, when we stopped to consider that we now quite voluntarily owned two Siamese and a donkey, we sometimes wondered about ourselves. If we turned to look at them we found they were invariably standing in the lane looking incredulously back at us.

One day, going out initially with Annabel, we passed a man on horseback who, after he'd got his frightened mare down on to all four feet again, said Funny little pet to have wasn't she, ha! ha! and rode on. An hour later, going the opposite way with Solomon and Sheba, we met him again. Hearing him coming, afraid that his horse might rear once more in the narrow lane, we grabbed the cats and jumped into the ditch. There, as he passed, we stood. Sheba scrambling over Charles's head with her back up. Solomon, who liked horses, complacently on my shoulder but with his tail anchored round my face so that it looked as if I was wearing a big black moustache. The man looked quite alarmed. Then, pulling himself together and probably assuring himself that if he humoured us he might make it even yet – 'Taking them for a walk?' he said.

We didn't care. We liked the cats. We liked Annabel, too, though we still weren't certain to what extent she liked us. Until, that was, the day I went out to see her after lunch and there, thinking nobody was about to shout at, she lay drowsily in siesta, outside her house in the sun. She had her front legs stretched before her like a sheepdog, as we'd seen her lie so often. Only this time there was no jumping up as I approached, nor even as I sat down cautiously in the straw beside her. Annabel, blinking contentedly in the sun, was half asleep. Annabel to my amazement, as I sat there stroking her nose and ears and wondering how fast I could get up if she decided to bite me, snorted dreamily, lowered her head and rested it lovingly on my shoulder.

There was no mistake about it. Once she lifted her head to reach down and bite her leg where a fly was tickling her. Again she lifted it when Charles – wondering from the silence, he said, whether I'd fallen in her feeding bowl and she'd eaten me – came and looked over the fence and nearly dropped at what he saw. Each time she drooped her lashes, snorted softly, and laid her head back on my shoulder to be stroked.

I told people about Annabel's responsiveness that day till they must have been tired of hearing it. I gave her peppermints. I went up to talk to her practically every half-hour. I saw myself achieving things unheard-of in the rapport between donkey – properly treated – and man.

It didn't take her long to blot that small beginning of a copybook. The next day, wandering up the lane with her in an atmosphere of mutual affection, on our own because Charles was spraying the grape-vine, minus my duffle coat because it was hot – and what need had I of protection now, when there was such a wonderful understanding between us? – Annabel bit me in the pants. A good hard nip like being caught by a pair of nutcrackers. Guess who did that? she enquired when I touched ground again, wobbling her underlip amiably at me *à la* Maurice Chevalier.

EIGHT

The Trouble with Tortoises

Our donkey apparently liked us. Solomon was mine to the extent that he alone was allowed to snuggle down with his head on my pillow when he and Sheba came into our bedroom in the mornings and if Sheba tried it on he bit her. Sheba would jump into a bath at any time to be with Charles, and when he worked at home she sat companionably on his desk like a paperweight, enquiring didn't he think she was pretty and making footmarks on his documents. The ingrate of the family – the one we never mentioned – was Tarzan the tortoise.

Tarzan, two years previously, had run away. Run was the operative word. Scarcely had we got to know him – scarcely, even, had the cats discovered which end to prod to make him work – than Tarzan bolted up the path one day while we were having lunch and vanished again till the following Spring. Tarzan, after that, had had a blue and white circle painted on his shell to make him more identifiable. Tarzan, we decided, thinking that might be what made him wander, should forthwith have a mate. We even decided on her name. Tosca we intended to call her. But there was a shipping strike on at the time. Tarzan wouldn't wait. By the time the boat came in and the Tortoises for Sale notice went up outside the local pet-shop, Tarzan, camouflaging himself presumably under a dandelion leaf, had gone again.

It was May when he disappeared and it was August – too late, we thought, to provide him with his Tosca at that time of year – when we discovered him again. Up on the hillside behind the cottage, where we'd gone quite by chance to call for Solomon, who as usual was missing when we wanted to go out. And there, as we shouted 'Tolly-wolly-wolly' and searched the neighbourhood with field glasses, for by this time he'd been missing for an hour and a half and we'd searched every thinkable place till we were exhausted, we discovered him. Not Solomon – whom we found eventually sitting conspicuously on the coalhouse roof saying he'd been there all the time though we knew jolly well he hadn't – but Tarzan. Standing on a rocky outcrop looking at us with his head out and a defiant expression on his face, and with the weather-worn remnants of the blue and white paint on his back to prove that he was ours.

How he'd got there in the first place was amazing, for behind the cottage garden was a ten-foot wall backing on the hill, and behind the cottage itself was an almost vertical stone-lined bank that one would have thought would have stopped an elephant let alone a tortoise. He spat at us when we took him back. Didn't want to live in the valley, he said, and we could tell from his expression he was mad. And so, seeing that a painted shell is useless when a tortoise takes to midsummer undergrowth or goes climbing above one's head, we fitted him with a ping-pong ball on the end of a long length of string tied round his waist on the principle of a marker buoy, offered him some bread and milk at which he withdrew his head and said he supposed we were trying to poison him now, and let him go. Outside the kitchen door where he immediately started out across the yard, which Charles was still in the process of paving, and got his ping-pong ball caught between a couple of stones.

We unhitched him from there, struggling away like a beleaguered Channel swimmer and spitting at us with disgust, and put him in the garden. There, for a few days while he learned the ropes, he stayed. Once, seeing the string pulled taut and Tarzan on the end doing his Channel-swimming act, I found he'd got the ping-pong ball anchored in the chrysanthemums. Shortly afterwards, seeing Tarzan struggling valiantly behind the dahlias, I looked to see what was holding him this time and found Solomon sitting on his string. Watching Tarzan's struggles on the end of it with the interest of an entomologist, but pretending, when he spotted me, that he hadn't a clue he was holding him up.

The third time it was the ping-pong ball I noticed, wrapped by its string round a rose tree. Three times round as if Tarzan had gone berserk and started walking in circles. But there was nothing berserk about that tortoise. Three times round for leverage that had been. When I trailed the string to where it ended in the Michaelmas Daisies, there was an empty red string waist-band and Tarzan once more had gone.

We never saw him again. He didn't appear the following Spring and we had, in fact, given him up as perished when, in the ensuing summer, we were invited out to supper by some people who lived up the hill a quarter of a mile away. They supposed, they said during the course of the evening, that we hadn't lost a tortoise? When we said we had as a matter of fact, nearly a year ago, they said they'd found one three weeks previously climbing up the hill. Two days following they'd seen him and the second day, fearing he might get run over, they'd taken him in and put him in their herbaceous border. Where, they said, he seemed to be pottering happily, came out to see them on occasion, and they'd grown quite fond of him.

It was Tarzan all right. The fact that he'd been found mountaineering was proof of that. But if he was going to keep leaving home and making for the heights; if he was happier when he got there – and the fact that he'd been pottering voluntarily in their flower-bed for weeks when he wouldn't stay five minutes in ours seemed proof enough of that – then they had, we said beneficently, better keep him.

They did. I, never having had Tarzan around long enough to strike up a bosom friendship with him, was content to let them. And Charles, after thinking it over for a fortnight, announced that he missed Tarzan and was going to ask for him back. When I said he couldn't, we'd *given* him to the people, he said he was going to lure him back. People had no right to other people's tortoises, he said, and if he went up there with a lettuce and Tarzan looked through the hedge at it he had as much right to pick him up as anybody. Tortoises, he said, were jolly interesting. Which was why the following week, to prevent Charles carrying out his threat of tortoise-napping and no doubt ruining our reputations for ever, I brought home two small baby tortoises.

Victoria and Albert we called them because at the time there was a move, quite rightly, to ban the importation of tortoises on account of bad conditions of transport, the petshop man said this might be the last consignment he'd have and Charles – quite brilliantly I thought, when I told him – said in that case they'd be museum pieces. We didn't know whether they were really a pair. According to our reference book the undershell of a male tortoise is concave and that of a female convex, but when I turned these two upside down in the petshop they were both, with my usual luck, flat. They were the only small ones they had, however, so I bought them in hope. And Charles and Solomon thought they were wonderful.

They lived temporarily, until Charles could make them a movable run in the garden, in a big cardboard box in the conservatory. Five feet by four, with a smaller cardboard box with a door in it in the corner for sleeping in, a couple of clumps of grass and a shallow dish of water. After we found that the cats were going into the box every time they passed the conservatory and drinking the water – he, said Solomon, lapping soulfully away amid the grass, was a Jungle Cat and he liked his water from a pool; she, said Sheba, didn't like silly old tortoises and drinking their water would annoy them – we put some chicken wire over the top.

Occasionally we put them out for exercise on the lawn, in a makeshift wooden frame that Charles had used the previous winter for growing anemones. It stopped them from straying but it was shallow and had no top, so that they were forever plodding round it one behind the other like circus elephants looking for a way out and Solomon, when he passed by and saw them in action, could never resist getting in and sitting bolt upright in the middle like a ring-master. Prodding them encouragingly when they stopped, or – if one of them did manage to find a foothold in a corner and by dint of terrific struggle get its chin over the edge – nipping excitedly out of the frame, lying flat on his stomach outside, and surprising them with a spidery black paw as their heads came over the top.

Eventually Albert did get out and we found him hiding under a nut tree. After that I balanced a tile on each of the corners of the run when they were exercising to prevent similar escapes and that – a strange wooden frame on our lawn, roof tiles set mysteriously on the corners and a Siamese cat in the middle prodding interestedly at something with his paw – was how people came to know we had tortoises. By opening the gate, country-fashion, and looking. That was also how we came to acquire another tortoise. Somebody rang up one day to say they'd found one wandering near the main road and could we – as they understood we kept tortoises – look after him while they enquired for his owner.

Charles, though he'd been found a mile away coming from quite a different direction, said it must be Tarzan returning home. It wasn't Tarzan because this one had a sort of frill to his shell and a broken hole in the edge whereby he'd obviously once been tethered. Moreover Tarzan, as I confirmed by ringing his current owners, was still in residence with them and had just eaten all the lettuce. But we kept him. Loose in the conservatory with a board across the doorway to stop him getting out. Albert and Victoria lived safe from his possibly predatory attentions in their cardboard box when they weren't out in their run. And there – once Charles got over his conviction that the new boy, left at large, would decapitate his grape-vine overnight by eating through the four-inch stem – they thrived. Paddling in their water-bowls, eating plums and lettuce – the big one, said Charles, had a remarkable bite; you could hear it like the action of a mechanical grabber, and after he'd bitten a piece of lettuce it was absolute seconds before he took the first slow chew and seconds after that before he took the next. He hoped, said Charles, that nobody would claim him. Tortoises were jolly interesting and next year, when he'd finished the goldfish pond, he was going to build a proper tortoise pit.

Which was why, eventually, we ended up with no tortoises at all. Three weeks after the arrival of Uncle Ernest, as we named him on account of the original Victoria also having had an Uncle Ernest, we went to Yorkshire for a couple of weeks. The cats went to Halstock. Annabel went to the farm where they gave her her first taste of oats and forecast more truly than they knew that she'd be coming back for more. A friend of ours agreed to feed the goldfish and the tortoises. We left them, as it was now September and cooler and we thought it safer like that in case anyone went in there, in the conservatory with the door shut. And the decline of our tortoise kingdom set in.

Our friend went down the next day to discover that Uncle Ernest, named more appropriately than we realised, had climbed in our absence on to Victoria and Albert's big box, tumbled through the chicken wire which was only loosely over the top, and was asleep with his head inside their sleeping quarters. Victoria and Albert, panic-stricken no doubt at his invasion, had clambered out of the box via the chicken wire which Ernest had pushed in and were now roaming exiled round the conservatory. Our friend, thinking Ernest would only oust them again if she put them back, decided to leave them as they were. Even then all would have been well had not she, the following weekend, had a cold, and a friend who was staying with her went down to feed the tortoises and there encountered, in all his naturalist's glory, Timothy, whom we'd asked to cut the grass.

Timothy it was – old Cleverpants who'd never kept a tortoise in his life – who decided along with our friend's friend that it was too hot for them with the conservatory door closed and left it open. Timothy who, when we arrived home to find the conservatory door ajar with a tomato enticingly in the opening but no tortoises, explained tearfully that he'd blocked the door with wood and stones and couldn't think how they'd gone. We could. Unless they are completely vertical, stones, as we knew from experience, can be climbed by tortoises as easily as butter. What was so unfortunate, too, was that it hadn't been too hot for them. Tortoises in their native islands enjoy a heat far greater than our conservatory could build up in September... But that, alas, was that.

We spent our first morning home on a tortoise hunt. Crawling round the garden searching in undergrowth and old stone walls while Timothy once more distinguished himself by telling me about the crocodiles. I was routing under the dahlias at the time, telling him that Charles had a theory that tortoises always headed south. Tarzan had gone south to his new home; Ernest was moving south when he was first picked up; hence I was looking first in this dahlia bed, south of the conservatory door, for the truants.

Timothy, as one naturalist to another, was most impressed. If I was in a jungle and came across a crocodile, he said by way of return (I appreciated the touch very much seeing as I was just then lying on my stomach with my hands in deep undergrowth in what is well-known adder country)... even if it was dead, did I know which way it would be facing? I didn't, I informed him, trying not to listen. Towards water, said Timothy triumphantly. Even if it was a skeleton – even if it was a hundred miles away when I found it – it would be pointing towards the water.

After that I continued the hunt on my feet and with gloves on, but we didn't find them. Victoria and Albert we were afraid might not survive. We were informed by a small girl, who could have told Timothy a thing or two about tortoises if she'd met him in time, that baby tortoises shouldn't be allowed to hibernate through the winter. Their insides weren't big enough, she explained, and we should keep them warm in their box and put down bread and milk for them when they felt hungry.

We'd better hurry up and find them, she advised us – and we only wished we could. Uncle Ernest, the cause of all the trouble, was big enough to look after himself and would probably emerge in the Spring to eat our lettuces as large as life. But Victoria and Albert – tucked, as we remembered them, side by side in their sleeping box like twin toy cars in a garage; emerging when the sun shone to eat their plums and take their baths; regarding us, when we picked them up, with inquisitively outstretched heads not the least like Tarzan and his spitting... Victoria on her first night with us, finding the door to the sleeping box by herself and going inside while Albert, with typical masculine blockheadedness, stuck his foreshell ostrich-fashion in a clump of grass and thought we couldn't see him... Tortoises do have character. We missed them very much.

NINE

The Sad Tale of Micawber

That wasn't the only setback we had that year. Back in the summer, with the tortoises newly with us, the mousing season in full swing and Annabel emerging by instalments from her baby coat, Charles had developed a passion for peanuts. Peanuts by the pound, since he never did anything by halves. The dustbin was filled with peanut tins, Charles was slapping his chest saying peanuts certainly had something. When I said they couldn't be good for him in such quantities and – by way of another approach – what on earth would the dustmen think when they tipped out all those tins, Charles, practically devastated by his own wit, said they'd think we were nuts.

He didn't laugh when his rash came up and the doctor said it was either the oil or all the salt in his system. For the next two months, he only had to get agitated or over-heated and it came up again within seconds, turning him a bright brick-red with bumps. It was during that period that we adopted a magpie, and in no time at all Charles' bumps were up like measles.

The magpie came to us from friends in town who'd found him sitting on their dustbin lid one morning. Tamed, they imagined, by someone who'd taken him from a nest in spring. Turned out to fend for himself when his owner got tired of him. Homeless but hopeful, with a strong predilection for humans despite the treatment he had received, Micawber didn't fancy fending for himself, and for a week, amply justifying the name they'd given him, he sat stolidly on their dustbin lid waiting for something to turn up.

Nothing did. Our friends fed him but wouldn't, as he obviously hoped they'd do, let him into their house. So he tried his luck with a neighbour, ate two rows of the neighbour's peas by way of introduction, flew frantically back to our friends when the neighbour chased him... He was now, they informed us in a phone call late that night, locked precautionally in their coal-shed. The owner of the peas was threatening to shoot him the moment he set eyes on him. Would we, for his own good, have him to live with us in the country?

Touched by his plight, we agreed. The cats were used to birds by now, we reasoned. Pheasants skimming the clearing in the wood with Solomon leaping salmon-like beneath them were a staple view from the cottage, but he never caught one. Sheba, going through the kitchen door, dropped to her stomach like a sharpshooter when she saw the blackbird in the yard, but it was only habit. The blackbird flipped his tail at her and went on eating. Sheba got automatically up as if from a curtsey and went on round the corner. Even the robin they besieged under the settee for an hour one day wasn't particularly worried. They sat there the whole of lunch-time – Sheba guarding one end like a Buckingham Palace sentry, Solomon peering intimidatingly under the other in the intervals of sharing the tomato soup, us thinking they'd mislaid a mouse until eventually they gave it up, wandered off, and, to our astonishment, a robin walked calmly from under the settee and started to look for crumbs. Nobody caught anybody any more. Micawber, we said when we heard of his troubles, would be quite all right with us.

Micawber was. It was Solomon who, within an hour of Micawber's arrival, was being rushed by car to the Vet's. Sheba, seeing us shut ourselves in the garage with a mysterious-looking basket and refuse to let her in, had climbed precipitously up to spy on us through a high outside window. Solomon, seeing her perched aloft like a mountain goat and inspired with his usual desire to imitate her, had tried to climb up to the sill himself and missed. Unknown to us there was a cloche beneath the window. And, as inevitably as everything happened to him, poor old Solomon fell through it.

His long black leg was ripped from top to bottom. Twelve stitches he had in it while, sick with remorse, we held him on the surgery table. Ten days he spent with his leg sewn up in a pathetic seam, turning our hearts every time we looked at him but not inconveniencing Solomon an inch. A fortnight we had Micawber and it seemed, in our extremity, like years.

Micawber said he was going to live in the garage. That was all right by us. We took down every cloche in sight. Charles put a ladder against the inside wall to give him a high, safe perch. We had to be careful, when we drove in, not to hit the ladder, otherwise the ladder immediately fell down and hit the car, but we soon got used to that. We put Micawber on the ladder by way of demonstration... Snag number one. Raised, presumably, in a low-hung cage, Micawber didn't like heights. He, he said, planing to earth so frantically you could practically see him mop his brow with relief when he got there, was a Ground Magpie. He took up residence on a box two feet off the ground, with a derelict door leaning against it one way which formed a sort of cave and a plank leaning against it the other way which formed a sloping gangplank and down this, to the detriment of Charles' rash, every time we or the cats approached he strolled grandly to meet us on foot.

Micawber liked having baths. Our friends discovered that when they saw him splashing earnestly in a garden puddle and we, to keep up the good work, provided him with a soup tureen. Snag number two. Micawber insisted on having that on the ground as well. Out in the drive in the sun, where he ducked and splashed like a grampus, sat blissfully on the edge of the tureen to dry, and we kept nerve-racked watch because if there was anything more vulnerable than a magpie who wouldn't fly it was a waterlogged magpie who couldn't.

That was how it appeared at first sight. Actually Micawber wasn't nearly as vulnerable as he looked. The moment a cat got within striking distance – sometimes, to make it even more hair-raising, the moment the cat actually struck

– and Micawber, throwing the business of being a Ground Magpie to the winds, was away. Not, unfortunately, very far. Flapping heavily to the sharp thin top of a beanstick with, a second later, Sheba threatening to leap up there as well and turn herself into a kebab. Fluttering precariously to the top of the garage door with Solomon, sewn-up leg or not, crouched beneath ready for a suicidal spring. Sitting, most dangerous of all, on the apex of the greenhouse, with the car nearby where we normally left it, Solomon and Sheba on the car roof preparing to dive in unison straight through the greenhouse glass, and Charles and I diving even faster to prevent them.

We nearly went mad over the car. We moved it a dozen times a day to a different part of the drive, but it was no use. If we left it nearer the lane it was nearer the bean rows too. Within seconds, the cats were on the roof crouched ready for the take-off and Micawber was sitting like a coconut on the nearest stick. If we left it nearer the garage it was correspondingly nearer the garage door with, this time, Micawber sitting seductively on the top of that. If we put it in the garage and shut the door Micawber immediately flew down, drooped his wings in the dust, huddled dejectedly against the door of what he said was his Only Home and, we gathered from his attitude, wept.

We practically wept, too. We netted the greenhouse and conservatory roofs to afford some protection to the cats. Resulting, needless to say, in the neighbours asking what the mackerel catch was like this morning. We took the netting off again when the cats weren't about in case Micawber got his legs entangled in the mesh and hurt himself. We enticed Micawber down to the cottage proper – away, we thought, from the perils of car and glass. Only to find that he then either sat interminably on the windowsills with the cats charging like Bengal Lancers at the panes from the inside or else kept walking affably at ground level through a kitchen door which had, if we didn't keep eternal watch on them, two equally affable Siamese behind it.

We felt absolutely besieged. We were besieged. That was obvious when we opened the door one day in a thunderstorm, peered apprehensively out to check whether Micawber was sitting on the doorstep, breathed a sigh of relief to see that he wasn't and prayed it might rain for a week – and there, in a flash, he was. Padding wetly to the edge of the coalhouse roof from his vigil under a lilac branch; flapping his wings to attract our attention; assuring us in his loud, harsh voice, while the rain ran off his tail in streams, that he was there and ready and watching.

He was there and ready and watching whatever we did, wherever we went, whatever the hour. At dawn on our bedroom windowsill. Waiting like a customer for the sales to open because, to prevent him coming in during the night, we now slept with the windows shut. At night, having abandoned the garage as too far removed from the centre of things, he watched from a nearby tree. Twice when we'd been away all day until late evening we crept down the path at dusk, admonishing one another not to make a noise, fond as ever of Micawber but hoping, in view of the problems he set us, that he might have given us up for lost this time and gone to live elsewhere. It was no use. Even at nightfall, with every other magpie in England asleep and snoring long before, Micawber was watching us. Down through the dusk he came, circling our shoulders like a bat, sitting on the greenhouse while we put the car away, huddling – the last we saw of him as we closed the kitchen door – a watching outline on the coalshed roof.

That one day was the last we ever saw of Micawber as we knew him. Our first feeling, when next morning he was missing from our bedroom windowsill, was one of relief. No Micawber waddling demoralisingly through the kitchen door the moment we opened it. No Micawber, when we looked round the corner, sitting picket-fashion in the porch. No Micawber, when we went up to feed Annabel, running flat-footedly after us with raucous squawks to play with our shoe-laces, pull at our sandal buckles or jump with a splash into her water-bowl.

It was Charles, growing worried, who found him, lying stunned in a nearby lane. It was nobody's fault that we could see. A rough, bumpy lane where nothing could possibly have speeded. A car lumbering up in bottom gear. Micawber wandering about the verge under the overhanging grass and flying up at the last moment, as was his wont with people and animals, only this time into a car... Sadly we took him in and fought to save him. Micawber fought too, but he died.

It sobered us all for a while. He'd been a nuisance, a danger to the cats and a chaser of other birds. Even the blackbird and the robin had deserted us, chased off so fast by Micawber when they came down to land that, scuttling about the yard on his big flat feet, he looked like a character in a silent film. It was, perhaps, for the best, but we wished it had been some other way. We wished Micawber had taken to the woods where, with no danger to anybody, he might be flashing still between the trees.

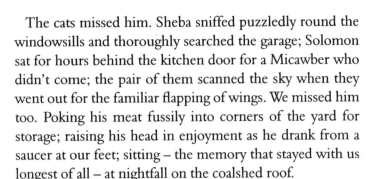

The cats missed him. Sheba sniffed puzzledly round the windowsills and thoroughly searched the garage; Solomon sat for hours behind the kitchen door for a Micawber who didn't come; the pair of them scanned the sky when they went out for the familiar flapping of wings. We missed him too. Poking his meat fussily into corners of the yard for storage; raising his head in enjoyment as he drank from a saucer at our feet; sitting – the memory that stayed with us longest of all – at nightfall on the coalshed roof.

It took another setback to return us to normal. Annabel, eating her way steadily through the summer, had chewed her hedge quite threadbare. From that, with Annabel's eye for effect, it had been a short step to putting her head through the gaps when people passed and reaching, seemingly ignorant of their presence, across the ditch for an odd, stray bramble leaf or an overlooked blade of grass. A touching sight, particularly now that she'd lost her baby coat completely and looked more defenceless than ever with her rounded limbs, minute feet, tiny little tail and the winsomest golden cowlick outside a toyshop. Quite unnecessary, of course, seeing that the paddock was big enough for a dozen donkeys, she had two meals a day and the neighbours fed her till she was fit to pop. But it got her buns and sympathy, and people – watched approvingly by Annabel over the side-fence once their backs were turned – coming to tell us she was hungry.

It also got her out. Annabel, leaning through the wires one day after an elusive dandelion, discovered that she could stretch the top strand up with her head, the middle strand out by leaning on it like a dray horse with her chest – and thereafter, having reduced them in a couple of performances to sagging loops, all she had to do was up with her head, through (stepping carefully) with her feet, and she was free. Running up the hill with Charles and me after her, Timothy racing to cut her off up a side-track, and the lot of us going round like Paul Revere.

Three times she did it in a day, each time at a different point, till the wires hung like Christmas bunting, Annabel was wild with excitement and we were practically flat on our backs. The next day we had to tether her. We didn't like it but there was no alternative until we could get home from town with additional poles and wire and reinforce her fence. She'd be all right, we told ourselves. We'd tethered her for days when we first had her, till we got her fence up. Apart from regularly winding herself up like a maypole till she was on ten feet of rope instead of thirty – plodding self-pityingly round being a Treadmill Donkey, we supposed, though we'd never seen her do it – she hadn't come to harm. Never, as we imagined her doing now, breaking a leg, or strangling herself, or tying herself to a tree. She just couldn't do it, we assured ourselves.

So we left her. Watching us downtroddenly from the middle of the field on the end of her rope. Practising, for the benefit of the day's passers-by, her Burgher of Calais look. And when we got back she'd done it. Hogtied herself so thoroughly in a corner of the paddock that at first we thought she was dead.

She lay there unmoving under the elder tree. Eyes closed, legs bound to her muzzle, coat damp with fear and sweat. Only later had we time to work out how she'd done it – rolling like a puppy in a dust patch with the rope tightening round her with every kick. Meanwhile, panic-stricken, we cut her loose, helped her to her feet, trembled to see that she limped and that, when she opened her mouth to trumpet, only a squeak came out.

She recovered all right. Water, a couple of peppermints, Charles massaging her legs while she leaned convalescently against his head and Annabel was as right as rain. Only Charles was back where he started from, with a flaming peanut rash.

TEN

Time to Take the Pledge

Ours, though sometimes we queried the fact, weren't the worst Siamese in the world. They didn't get drunk, for instance. Like the cat belonging to one of our friends who, enjoying a sherry one night before dinner, put it down by her chair while she read the paper and, when she picked up the glass a moment or two later, found it empty. It gave her the shock of her life, she said, particularly as she was alone in the house. It gave her an even bigger one when she looked apprehensively round and there behind her chair, regarding her from behind the paw he'd used to dip the sherry from the glass and was now licking to extract the last lingering flavour, was her seal-point Siamese Pinocchio. He absolutely leered at her, she said. When she tried to make him stand upright he couldn't. She laid him on her bed. He leered at her again she said, awestruck at the memory, and then he passed out for two solid hours.

They didn't push people in pianos, like a Siamese we knew called Soraya. She, a complete disgrace to her name, leapt on the back of a tuner one day when he was looking into a Bechstein Grand, laid him flat with surprise in the works, and fled. The worst of that was that when the tuner came out again he wouldn't believe a cat was responsible. He'd heard a terrible Yell, he kept insisting. And as there was nobody else in the house at the time but Soraya's owner, undoubtedly she went down in his works report as having done it. Had a sudden mad moment and pushed him in the piano.

Ours weren't particularly temperamental, either. Sheba wouldn't eat if you were looking at her, Solomon created hell and howled if, summer and winter, I didn't wear a particular skirt he liked at night so that he could sit on it, but that was normal Siamese behaviour. Not, for instance, like a cat we knew called Sabre, who had such attacks of nerves when people rang the doorbell that his owners disconnected it. After that people used the knocker. That made him nervous too, so they took the knocker off. A rather drastic step, but the alternative was a cat who spent most of his time hiding traumatically under the gas-stove. So, following complaints from callers who now couldn't make themselves heard at all, they'd connected the doorbell button to a series of lights placed strategically in the hall, the kitchen and over the television set. Red they were, going on and off in ghostly silence. An ingenious invention it was, too. Save for the fact that, apart from their effect on human beings, the last we heard of him Sabre was staring traumatically at the lights as well.

Annabel, similarly, wasn't a particularly wicked donkey, compared with the tales we heard of donkeys who bit, donkeys who kicked carts out of shafts and the donkey who lay at the roadside and pretended to be dead. Father Adams told us that one, and if we'd thought we were unique in introducing a donkey into the valley that, we understood, was where we were wrong. William his name were, Father Adams informed us reminiscently, and sixty years earlier William had been a familiar sight plodding up and down the hill with his little ironmonger's cart. Until the day when, it seemed, William had stumbled at the bottom of the hill, sagged dramatically to his knees and lain down, saucepans and all, in the gutter.

Considerable fuss had been made of William. Once they'd discovered he wasn't dead he'd been lifted wiltingly from the shafts, given whisky in hot water, led gently up the hill when he recovered while the villagers hauled up his cart. The Vet could find nothing wrong with him. He'd lived for another twenty years. What had caused him to collapse initially no one knew. Except that thereafter William collapsed so often at the same spot, to be revived only by whisky and water or the sound of his cart being dragged up the hill by volunteers, that in the end his owner gave up bringing him down. William waited seraphically at the top, the ironmonger trudged blisteringly up and down with a basket, and William never fainted again. You couldn't put one over on a donkey, Father Adams advised us repeatedly when he saw us with Annabel.

We'd learned that for ourselves. Annabel's gate, for instance, fastened with a strap. Annabel playing with the strap when we were there was one thing – nuzzling at the end, tossing her head good-humouredly at us through the fence, indicating that *she* knew this was the way out and what about a walk. Annabel going at it when our backs were turned was another. We spotted her one day when, in leisurely mood, we were watching swallows on our telephone wire through binoculars. Four swallow fledglings they were, sitting obediently in a row while their parents hunted for food. There was an obvious pattern to the business. Absolute silence while Mum and Dad hunted; a fluttering of wings like a Parisian chorus as Mum and Dad returned; shrieks, gaping beaks and clamours for more as Mum and Dad stuffed the food down their throats; and finally, quiet again as Mum and Dad took off for the next instalment. What intrigued us was the bird sitting on the wire alongside them – fluttering his wings, opening his beak, stretching out his neck at the appropriate moments but quite obviously not a swallow. He, announced Charles, inspecting him knowledgeably through the binoculars, was a whitethroat and obviously one of the valley's wide boys. Trying to horn in on feeding time but the parent birds weren't having any. Wasn't Nature marvellous? demanded Charles enthusiastically. Weren't these creatures characters? Whereupon he brought the glasses downwards from the telephone wire, swept them by way of interest across the paddock, and lit quite by accident upon another character. Annabel – with no one, so she thought, to see her working doggedly away at her strap.

There was nothing playful about this effort. Teeth bared, head jerking purposefully from side to side, Annabel was tugging away like Houdini. We confined her with chain and padlock after that. To offset any feeling of frustration that might give her – she must, said Charles, have wanted to be with us otherwise she wouldn't have been doing it – we gave her longer walks and time in the garden.

What Annabel wanted was to be out. Initially, at any rate, her one idea when she achieved that object was to dash past the cottage, half-way up the hill, and hover. Feeding blissfully on the roadside, lifting her head occasionally to see if we were watching, running a skittish few steps when we tried to approach her, and coming back like the clappers when a car came round the corner.

Time in the garden altered that, however. Time in the garden – beginning with half an hour on the days we went to town, when she was allowed at the kitchen door in the early morning, given bread and honey as a treat, and usually had to be pushed Atlas-fashion back to her paddock while we sweated on the top line about the hour – rapidly became the criterion of Annabel's existence.

It grew, when occasion permitted, to be several hours. Any time she got out of the paddock now, either by crawling under the wire or the more direct method of meeting us at the gate as we opened it and pushing past us like a steam-roller and Annabel was *chez nous*. Wheeling smartly up the drive. Chewing familiarly at one of Charles' plum trees. Rubbing her bottom appreciatively on a Cox's Orange – a low one under which her back fitted perfectly and it wasn't just that she pushed it from side to side, said Charles despairingly; it went up and down as well. And finally, Mecca of Meccas, achieving the kitchen.

When Annabel first discovered the existence of the kitchen she was quite overawed by it. All that Food, you could see her thinking as she stood, overwhelmed, outside. The place where the bread and honey came from, and the apples and chocolate biscuits. Even when she'd come down the garden like a tornado – a nip at the plum tree, a boomps-a-daisy on the apple and three times round the lawn for luck – she still, when she reached the kitchen door, sobered down to respectful silence.

Not for long, however. Within a day or so a small white nose was cautiously nudging the door open. Soon a familiar head was coming tentatively inside. Within a short time after that the Winged Mercury attitude with flattened-back ears, eyes like marbles and outstretched neck as, ready to run, she reached round the corner to the kitchen table, had changed to a sort of vacuum-sweeping action as, as nonchalantly as you liked, she nosed appraisingly over its surface. And eventually, to Charles' delight, she was coming right into the kitchen. Looking knowledgeably for apples in the dish, hunting familiarly for carrots in the vegetable rack, hitting the refrigerator a resounding thwack with her bottom as she turned. Who, said Charles gazing proudly upon her, would believe we'd tamed a donkey to that extent?

Nobody, said Sidney decidedly. 'Twas bad enough when everywhere you went you was tailed by a couple of cats. When you opened a kitchen door and came face to face with a donkey, 'twas time to take the pledge.

Some people apparently felt that way when they saw her wearing a sou'wester – an innovation of Charles, who put it on her one day for a joke, discovered that she liked it, and when it rained Annabel could now be seen plodding happily round the garden like Grace Darling. We felt like taking it ourselves when as the next item on Annabel's list of achievements with which to surprise us, she came boundingly into season.

We didn't know much about donkeys. Only that we'd been told she shouldn't be ridden till she was three, shouldn't be bred from till she was three, and in our innocence we naturally assumed she wouldn't grow up till she was three either. The discovery, after our Arcadian interlude of prancing on the lawn and dallying in the kitchen, that she was marriageable at a year and we didn't have a seraglio ready to put her in was one of our tenser moments in donkey keeping.

Charles went round strengthening the fence as if for an attack by Indians. Annabel followed him with a coy swish of her tail saying Funny if one came over from Weston, wouldn't it be. Father Adams said he wouldn't worry if he was us, his father never locked 'em up, and countered it immediately with the recollection of a cart-horse that had come clattering down the lane one night, jumped a six-foot hedge and given his father's mare twins. And at two in the morning we were roused by a mysterious noise up the valley.

We were expecting it, of course. A jack! cried Charles, who'd been lying there listening for one since midnight. Quick! I said, having been lying there with even deadlier visions of a carthorse coming down the hill. Even so Annabel was up before us. She had heard it too and wasn't it exciting? she demanded, coming to meet us at her gate.

As a matter of fact it was a cow. Bellowing for its calf in a field up the valley, as we realised when it called again. It might have been a boy though, Annabel snuffled happily. One might be coming any moment now and she was going to stay up and Wait for him, she called after us as we plodded back to the cottage. One might indeed. Half an hour on our sleepless pillows imagining jacks creeping down the lane every time a branch creaked and we were up again. Getting out the car. Locking Annabel in the garage. And twenty minutes later getting up once more because she was up there banging paint tins around.

Twice since then she'd been in season. No jack had so far materialised. On the strength of the opinion of the Vet who said he didn't suppose one would either at that time of year after a hard day's work on the sands, we no longer locked her in the garage at such times; we just lay awake and worried instead. Annabel had achieved a lot one way and another. What we hadn't got her to do was work.

We'd made one or two attempts. We'd failed to get the bracken off the orchard in time for her to graze up on our own land. Charles was building his fishpond and perpetually anticipating getting round to the orchard next week. Sidney said the snakes was worse than ever this year and we could count he out. I went up there with a hook and disturbed a wasp's nest, reporting it to Charles who thereupon completed the circuit by saying he'd deal with the wasp's nest next week too. But we'd lent her out to the neighbours.

Only for an hour or so, we stipulated, as they led her pleasurably away to eat down their weeds. We couldn't let our donkey go for long... She usually went for considerably less. Hardly, it seemed at times, had her demure little rump disappeared round the corner of the lane accompanied by a jovial neighbour than her demure little nose was coming back round it in the other direction accompanied by a neighbour who held her rigidly at arm's length, and was cool towards us for days after a recital of what she'd done.

Knocking down a rockery was one of the charges laid against her. Scratching her bottom on it, said its owner. The more he'd pulled her away and showed her the dandelions the more she'd backed stubbornly against a big loose stone and scratched, the rockery had come down like a pack of cards and *she*, he said, his voice rising indignantly at the thought of it, had looked reprovingly at *him*.

Eating an asparagus bed had been another accusation. Four years to grow and gone like a row of candles, announced her borrower on that occasion, handing her rope to us and departing as if he were sleep-walking, with never a backward glance.

Jumped off a five-foot bank was another report and when we enquired worriedly had she hurt herself, were her legs all right, had she *fallen*, Mr Smithson said bitterly not on his nelly. Took off like a ruddy chamois, he said. Straight off the ruddy bank-top, straight into the air, and straight down into the cucumbers.

Privately we thought she'd been frightened. Donkeys didn't jump, we said, examining her anxiously for damage when he'd gone. Annabel wouldn't leap off a *bank*. Annabel underlined every word we said with downcast eyes and intimated that Mr Smithson had pushed her. Only a day or two later did she forget herself and not only leapt off another bank just to show us but jumped a gate as well. A broken-down gate admittedly, only two feet high in the middle, but – seeing us shut it to keep her out of somebody's garden – she soared over it and into the garden like a hunter. Ought to put she in for the National, said the postman, and to let he know when we did it.

Annabel didn't eat down the nettles, didn't work – looked like never working so far as I could see, since Farmer Pursey said she wouldn't be obedient till she had a bridle. At the same time he patted her head and said we couldn't put one on her yet though could we, her little mouth was too tender; and Charles nearly fainted at the thought. It seemed a wonderful idea, therefore, when she was asked to help at the village fête. The forerunner, we forecast happily, of her being asked to help at lots of fêtes when people heard of it. Carrying the lucky dips, giving little rides to toddlers, going round with a box on her back collecting money for good causes. No need for a bridle for that, we assured ourselves. Not on the Rectory lawn.

We were always assuring ourselves of something and discovering our mistake. There we were a fortnight later, stopped in the middle of the village, late already for the fête and with Annabel looking down the drains. Not – as we remembered too late – having been in that part of the village before she'd never seen a drain, and drains, she said, were Interesting. She peered down every one she came to; it looked, said Charles, as if we were stopping at lamp-posts with a dog; to combat anybody getting the impression that that was why we were stopping with a donkey we gathered round and peered intently down the drains as well... Looking for Christmas? enquired Sidney, whizzing precipitously past on his bike.

There we were at a later stage outside the telephone box on the village green while Annabel ate some bread. On the ground where someone had thrown it for the birds, but she couldn't waste it, she said decidedly. Not when she was Hungry, she protested, pulling stubbornly back on her lead when we tried to get her away. Not while there was somebody in the telephone box either, with the receiver in her hand, glaring furiously at us through the glass. She glowered at us, we smiled embarrassedly in return... Heard anything interesting lately? called Sidney, as he sailed exuberantly back.

There we were, eventually, at the fête. Annabel, at the Rector's suggestion, wearing her sou'wester. The sun incongruously shining. The children milling round for the lucky dips which she carried in a sack on either side. The Rector beaming happily upon the festive scene.

He didn't beam for long. Five minutes or so of standing still while people fussed around her and Annabel moved off on a tour of inspection. Determinedly, carrying the dip bags, and accompanied by a trail of children. Nothing Charles or I could do could stop her. She met up with Miss Wellington, who was running a competition with a bucket of water with a half-crown in it. (You dropped in a penny. If you covered the half-crown you won it. If you didn't the penny went to the organ fund and Miss Wellington, with the doctor muttering darkly about her rheumatism every time he passed, skittishly fished it out.) Annabel drank the water.

She wandered to the handwork stall and, while we struggled to turn her away, looked inexorably over the contents. Nothing of interest there, said Annabel. But there was when we moved on. Water from her whiskers on a set of embroidered doileys. She found the home-made cake stall, regarded it steadfastly till someone gave her one and then the stall had to be cleared in a hurry because Annabel wanted the lot.

Nothing serious in any of it, mind you, unless you counted her making a camel-mouth at the lady who removed the walnut cake she particularly fancied, and Annabel wouldn't really have bitten her. Just, said the Rector, that she was a little young for a fete perhaps, and excited by the crowds. Just, said Charles, as we trudged deflatedly home with her long before the end of the fete, that she did it purposely, like the cats... Annabel's trouble really, of course, was that, like the Elephant's Child, she was filled with curiosity. En route for home, near Sidney's cottage, we met a cat sitting on a garden wall. Blue Persian as it happened, as against the Siamese to which Annabel was accustomed.

She stopped and gravely studied it. Why was it *blue*, why didn't it have *points*, why was it round instead of gawky like the ones we had at home... you could see Annabel's ears whipping about like semaphore flags while she thought it out. Cars came past and stopped. People looked out and clucked at her. Sidney came out to see what the fuss was about. 'Lumme,' he said, seeing us posed like pillars of salt for the third time that afternoon. 'Thee'st been struck by lightnin' or somethin'?'

ELEVEN

Two's Company

It was in October that our moment of truth caught up with us. All the summer Miss Wellington had been campaigning for a companion for Annabel. All the summer we'd been assuring her, first that Annabel didn't need a companion, and then, as summer drew to its close, that maybe we'd think about one for the winter.

A borrowed one, we said as the idea grew upon us. One from the local seaside, just to stay with Annabel through the desolate months when there weren't so many of her friends about. A donkey mare, we firmly informed Miss Wellington who, with stars in her eyes, was already envisaging Annabel roaming a wintry paddock cheek to cheek with a he-donkey and in due course – in the Spring, said Miss Wellington romantically, disregarding the fact that donkeys take a lot longer than that – having a little donkey foal. Maybe we could have Annabel's Mum, said Charles one day with inspiration – and what, when one thought of it, could be nicer? A touching reunion; the pair of them nuzzling secrets together in their stable on winter nights; Mum, a trained and conscientious beach donkey, teaching Annabel to be obedient, which was more than we looked like achieving ourselves in a month of Sundays...

Without more ado it was arranged. We drove over to see her owner. Sure he remembered us, he said. Sure we could have Mum for the winter. We liked donkeys, did we? he enquired, entering us efficiently on the back of an envelope and promising she'd be over in October. We went off on holiday with the idea of Mum still a comforting figure in the future. Came back and looked for the tortoises. Annabel, with memories of the oats they'd given her at the farm, got through her fence twice in a week and was found each time, with her trunk metaphorically packed, waiting hopefully outside the Purseys' gate.

Mum wouldn't have that, we scolded her as we brought her captively home. Mum wouldn't have that, we assured her as we avoided a donkey making camel-mouths at us while we mended her fence. Mum certainly wouldn't have that, we said, when a day or so later she deliberately rolled on a bucket of ashes and squashed it. Her ashes, weren't they? snuffled Annabel, rolling determinedly backwards and forwards like a rolling pin. And so they were, and perhaps we should have been quicker at emptying them on her rolling patch, and maybe it was our fault that when we got the bucket out from under her it was flatter, said Charles regarding it with awe, than a water-lily leaf. But the next day, quite without excuse, she rolled the watering-can flatter than a water-lily leaf too. Too many oats, we said. Not enough discipline, we said. Where, said Miss Wellington like the voice of Nemesis, was Annabel's mother?

She was right. October, with its bonfires and garden tidying and Charles working diligently away at the goldfish pond, had gone with the wind without our realising it. Annabel's Mum had gone with the wind too, as we discovered when we rang the donkey-man. She was up in Wiltshire, he informed us apologetically. He'd lost the envelope, we hadn't rung, a farmer had taken her for winter board with the rest of the donkeys... He'd got a jennet or two left behind though, he suggested helpfully. He could let us have one of those if we liked. And, so help me, we said yes.

When the jennet arrived a week later I was in bed. Suffering from a cold, with a gale blowing outside, the cats sitting side by side on top of me and Charles, as husbands usually do when their helpmeets are unable to reply, holding conversation with me up the stairs. 'You there?' he called solicitously, following with an enquiry as to whether I'd like some coffee. 'You there?' he called a little later. This time to the effect that the papers had come and where were the sweets for Timothy. 'You there?' came the familiar cry a moment or two after that. And, while I gathered my strength to enquire where he thought I was with a cold like this, up a perishing pine tree – 'The jennet's come!' he said.

I wasn't there very much longer. Five minutes later, with the jennet in the paddock and the van grinding irrevocably away up the hill, Charles came up the stairs. He hoped he'd done the right thing in taking it in, he said. It wasn't one of the little chestnut ones we'd anticipated; it was black. It wasn't very small; he reckoned I could ride it. It wasn't a she either, he revealed, the story developing by leaps and bounds with the intensity of a Victorian melodrama. It was a he by the name of Henry. The man said it was definitely a jennet, though, he'd be all right with Annabel, and he'd be coming to fetch him back in March.

A few more salient points like that, such as that Annabel only came up to Henry's middle, Henry appeared to be hungry and Annabel was kicking him – Annabel had long since eaten all the leaves off her trees up to Annabel height; Henry, according to Charles, was now going methodically round the paddock eating them off up to Henry height, and that was why Annabel was kicking him – and I was up all right. Staggering up to the paddock in pyjamas, duffle coat and gumboots to see for myself. Greeting a neighbour, whom I met inevitably because I was in the lane on Sunday afternoon in pyjamas and with my hair on end, with what I hoped was a nonchalant smile. Falling for Henry the moment I saw him.

Henry was big and black and sleek with a tail that fell like a waterfall. Henry's mane had been clipped like a horse's but, presumably to take some sort of trapping, a stiff black tuft had been left on top like the scalp lock of a Mohawk Indian. Henry was a jennet all right – you could see it, though only faintly, in the sturdiness of his legs and the slightly long black ears. But Henry was very handsome. That Annabel realised it too was obvious from the way she was standing by his side. Coyly; femininely; emphasising with unmistakable deliberation the fact that she indeed only came up to his middle. Helen and Paris, said Charles, forgetting his apprehension in his admiration of the scene. Annabel and Henry, I said with equal pride. I put out my hand to pat him, and Annabel immediately kicked Henry.

Annabel kicked Henry a lot. Determinedly but coquettishly, obviously fully aware of her feminine prerogative. She kicked him when we tried to stroke him. She was our donkey – he wasn't Allowed, she said, pushing imperiously between us and Henry and giving a few sharp back-kicks to emphasise the fact. She kicked him when we gave him titbits. She was our donkey and everything was Hers, she said, interposing her bottom in so many directions at once to fend him off that at times she appeared to be doing the Charleston. We evolved a system of holding sugar or a piece of bread close to the fence for her and then, while she was eating it, surreptitiously handing another piece over her back to Henry. Henry, reaching equally surreptitiously over her to get it, soon cottoned on. So, unfortunately, did Annabel. Following a trick or two like that she only had to see the shadow of a hand pass over her head and Annabel kicked capriciously behind and clocked Henry on principle. She knew he was there and that'd teach him not to Sneak, she snorted into her bread and honey.

It wasn't that she didn't like Henry. She just intended to be boss. The first night he was there, for instance, Henry moved into the shelter at dusk as if it was his right. It was too small for him, being only Annabel size, so he stood up all night as if he was in a sentry box with his rump inside and his head and forefeet out. Annabel, presumably under the impression he was standing there on guard and had his eye on her, didn't attempt to throw him out that evening. She stood up too, under a nearby tree, looking warily across at him, pretending she was grazing, and working out a plan. There must have been a plan because the next night it was Annabel who got there first and stood Horatio-like in the doorway while Henry loitered under the tree. And the next night and the next night, till Henry got the idea it was Annabel's shelter and stopped trying to go in there himself, Annabel Frrmphed triumphantly and said she should think so, too – and the next thing we saw, going out one night with a torch to check on the position to date, was Henry standing under his tree and no sign of Annabel at all. Annabel, ascendancy established, had given up keeping guard. Annabel, when we looked inside her house, was back where she belonged. Asleep flat out in the straw with her hooves crossed, her cowlick over her eyes and a pout of triumph on her small white mouth. The only concession to watchfulness being that she had her head towards the door.

Banned from the shelter, kicked when he spoke to us – kicked, according to the neighbours, even when he spoke to them and the people up the lane said the way Annabel ate ginger-cake now was a revelation – Henry might have been excused for developing a temper. He did in fact kick me a couple of times. On account of their jealousy we fed them separately – oats and hay for Annabel outside her shelter, oats and hay for Henry under his tree – and still they squabbled. Annabel marched over to Henry's heap and said it was better than hers, Henry moved over to Annabel's heap and said very well he'd eat that, Annabel charged back in a towering temperament snorting That was hers as well, she'd have the Law on him... Feeding time in the paddock was less a matter of eating than of Annabel and Henry playing musical chairs and, when they stopped, Annabel standing truculently over whichever pile she fancied at the moment, snorting and threatening to kick Henry off.

At first Henry, being a gentleman, gave in to the lady and went. Eventually Henry, goaded beyond endurance, began to kick back in retaliation. Never, even then, to land. Simply thrashing out in a powerful arc to show her he could, if he wanted to, kick her over the cottage; missing her deliberately on account of she was a girl by a good six inches; and having no effect on Annabel the Wilful at all. Only on me, whom he kicked by accident in the stomach.

I thoughtlessly went too close behind him; he, lashing out in what was meant to be a warning to Annabel, caught me amid-ships and laid me flat; and Charles (it was one of my more off-moments in donkey-keeping) picked me winded from the grass and cheerily said No Harm Done. Fortunately not, as Henry didn't wear shoes. I only had a bruise the size of a plate on my stomach, and an assurance from Charles that he'd had that many a time playing cricket. Which I took leave to doubt because I used to play cricket myself at school and we never caught balls on our stomachs. Though, as Sidney said when he heard about it, you never knew with the Gaffer.

After that I stood carefully on one side when I was with Henry. Even then I got caught one night when I patted him on the rump at dusk; he thought it was Annabel up to her tricks and kicked out, and the bag of bread I was holding soared straight into the middle of the field. A magnificent, arching goal-kick, with the top of the bag still left in my hand. I ought to be more careful, said Charles reprovingly. Silly playing at donkeys when I didn't know how to kick,

Donkey Work

said Annabel, standing watching me from outside her house with a wisp of hay in her mouth. Wooooh! said Solomon apprehensively from his post by the fence. Which was how I felt myself.

Henry seemed liable to put me into orbit any day but there was no question of his hurting Annabel. That, illustrated by the way he carefully kicked to miss her and turned a paternal eye on the cats, was why we kept him. Not only did we have a feeling that, jealousies apart, Henry liked Annabel. We had no doubt about the fact that Annabel liked Henry.

We watched sometimes in the paddock when there was neither food nor us on their minds. Wherever Henry grazed, Annabel grazed as well. Not kicking now because the grass was free, but standing like a prim small toy at his side. Wherever Annabel wandered Henry followed, trailing amiably after her like a clumsy guardian giant. Occasionally we even saw them in a corner rubbing noses.

She kicked him, she grazed with him. She kicked him, she rubbed noses with him. The paddock grass vanished like snow in summer before Henry's formidable hooves and Henry's enormous mouth. The hay and oats vanished like snow in summer, too, what with Henry eating three times as much as Annabel and the pair of them eating twice as much as they normally would on account of rivalry. One moment we wondered whether we should ever have taken Henry. The next, smoothing his big black nose when Annabel wasn't looking, we assured him we wouldn't be without him. The one thing we could congratulate ourselves on was – as we were only agreeing with Miss Wellington one weekend when we'd had Henry with us for

110

a fortnight – that Annabel was no longer lonely, and that she'd not since run away. I can see us saying it now, leaning on the paddock gate with Henry and Annabel plodding companionably towards us. Like Dignity and Impudence, said Miss Wellington ecstatically.

I can see us a little later. Taking Annabel for her first walk since we'd had Henry. Leaving him regretfully behind because we weren't quite certain how he'd handle on a walk with Annabel as yet, but assuring him that we'd take him, too, before long. Touched to the heart by the way he ran up and down the fence at being parted from Annabel, calling to her from the gate and watching her anxiously till she was out of sight. Quite unlike Annabel, who capered skittishly up the lane, never looked back at him once, and greeted him on her return with a vastly superior snuffle.

I can see myself at three the next morning, too, rolling down the stairs to answer the telephone. Wondering what catastrophe had hit the family now. Shivering unbelievingly in the cold November night while the riding mistress informed me that Annabel and Henry had eloped. They were over there with her, two miles away. She'd captured Annabel and tied her to the kitchen door. Henry was running about in the road and wouldn't be rounded up. She was in her pyjamas. And would we please come over at once.

TWELVE

The Elopement

We felt like Henry V before Agincourt that night, with everybody so patently abed and sleeping as we sped at panic stations through the lanes. Everybody, that was, except us and Miss Linley, keeping vigil in her pyjamas on the main road.

It was the moonlight, we thought, that had done it. The clear bright moonlight shining enticingly on the road that led out of the valley, and Henry made restless by the fact that Annabel had been taken for a walk and fancying one himself.

The moonlight, the night before, had enticed another local pony from his field. He, too, had broken out and gone clattering down the road and woken Miss Linley who, alone perhaps in the whole district, was attuned to hearing horses in her sleep. He, she said, had been going too fast. Almost before she was out of the house and running after him, he'd run into a lorry and been killed.

That was why she was worried about Henry. That was why we were worried, too. That; the fact that he didn't belong to us so that we had an added responsibility as his guardians; and the heart-sinking realisation that once we did succeed in rounding him up we were faced with the prospect of leaving the car at the stables and walking him and Annabel the two miles home.

There was an air of unreality about the journey. The silence; the silver landscape in which nothing moved; the cardboard shadows of the trees across the lanes. Miss Linley, waiting by the roadside in a hastily pulled-on coat, seemed more like part of a dream. So – except that it was more like part of a nightmare – did a familiar voice shouting advisorily over the wall when she heard us that she was Tied up in Here and not to believe them if they said she Wasn't. And the lights, following that sleep-shattering outburst, that immediately went on like lighthouse lanterns in bedroom windows all around us. And Miss Linley telling us she'd managed to round Henry up after all and chase him into the Plaices' drive and shut their gates behind him.

We could have fallen on her neck with relief. We haltered Henry, who by this time had spotted a mare and foal in the Plaices' paddock and was gazing fascinatedly at them over the fence. We led him back to the stables, where Annabel was standing unrepentantly by the kitchen door in the first professionally put-on halter she'd ever had, looking exactly like a circus Shetland.

Wasn't she a poppet? demanded Miss Linley. We'd never think, would we, that when she caught her the little minx wouldn't move out of the road, and she'd had to call her mother down to help, and between them they'd practically carried her into the yard.

Neither, seeing her standing there so innocently, would anybody guess what else she'd done. Annabel at home was most particular. She never used the garden as a lavatory and only certain parts of her paddock. Annabel at the stables, to show her opinion of having a halter put on her, had gone as far into the kitchen as her rope would allow and misbehaved on the rug.

Miss Linley only laughed. They might as well stay in her paddock for the night now, she said. We could fetch them back tomorrow.

We enjoyed that part of it very much. The walk over to the stables on a morning that was more like spring than autumn. The sight of Henry lying stretched out in the paddock when we got there – resting, we supposed, after his night's adventures. The sight of Annabel – after an initial shock when we couldn't see her at all and thought she was missing again – stretched out similarly a short distance away. Almost invisible in the grass, obviously imitating Henry – wasn't it marvellous, we said, the way they'd taken to one another? Even – if one overlooked the shock they'd given us – the way they'd run away together, just like Hansel and Gretel.

We went home pack-horse style. Henry first, led by Charles and walking as ponderously as a police horse up the busy main road. Annabel behind, led by me and for the first time in her life acting neither like a yo-yo nor a sheet anchor on the end of her rope but walking equally ponderously in the rear in imitation of Henry. Charming it was, apart from an undoubted resemblance to a procession en route for the sands with us in the role of donkey boys. Really quite touching when we turned off the road into the valley and whenever Henry disappeared round a bend ahead Annabel ran like mad till she had him in sight again, while every now and again Henry himself stopped and turned deliberately round to make sure that Annabel was following.

We tethered them in a nearby field while we carried out repair work on the paddock. Inspiring though it was to see the latest development in their relationship, we could work a whole lot faster without the prospect of being kicked to the boundary if anything upset Henry, or of Annabel's latest little trick of leaning innocently on the fence wire while we were stringing it so that when she stood upright again it hung in loops and was – as she archly demonstrated by lifting it with her nose – absolutely useless.

All day long it took us. Strengthening the fence. Enlarging Annabel's house with the help of Timothy so we could lock them in at night. Roofing it with hurdles and a huge tarpaulin and filling it with straw. We brought back Heloise and Abelard. Put them in the house and fed them. Fastened them in as it was now nightfall. Looked through the hurdle door a little later to see Henry stretched out like a great black sultan in the straw and Annabel contentedly eating hay...

If only it could have continued like that. Annabel and Henry together for the winter. Miss Wellington happy at last. Ourselves sleeping blissfully at night with the thought of all our animals under lock and key. But the next night Henry broke out again. At dusk this time, before we'd even thought of shutting them in. Fortunately we heard the twanging of the paddock wires as he squirmed his way through and the sound of his hoof-beats going like coconuts on the hill. Fortunately the wiring was too complicated this time for anybody but an expert to get through it and Annabel was unable to follow him. Even more fortunately, as we panted desperately up the hill in his wake Farmer Pursey came round the corner in his land-rover and headed him back to the valley.

That was the end as far as Henry was concerned. Obviously he was a bolter and had escaping in his blood. Keep him, said Farmer Pursey, and not only would we never, however much we wired the place, fence him in, but he'd teach Annabel his tricks as well. Keep him, he said, and we'd probably have the pair of them killed. What Henry wanted was exercise to tire him out, not mooning round a field with Annabel.

So Henry went back to his owner. To our regret because we liked him. With such regret on Miss Wellington's part that she turned up two days later with the news that she'd seen several donkeys in a field from a bus window and had got off at the next stop to enquire. The man, she said, was perfectly willing for us to have one of his little donkeys to keep Annabel company, and when Charles said he bet he was – one of his little bolters too, he expected, and if anybody brought any more donkeys here we were emigrating to Jamaica – she went off us again for days.

Annabel, to our surprise, showed no concern at all. She snorted contentedly when we fed her, lingering gloatingly over her bowl with the intimation that it was all hers wasn't it and nobody to have to share it with. She pranced so joyously out at Charles when he unbarred her door in the mornings that there was no mistaking the inference that there was Much more room for fun now, with old Big Feet out of the way. Despite the morning when she'd trailed Henry up the valley, acting as though the skies would fall if she lost sight of him for an instant, there was such an air of Things being like they Used to be, Annabel having Triumphed, and it was Hoped we realised now who was the best donkey around here, that we wondered if we'd been mistaken in taking him on in the first place.

The cats, who'd kept strictly to the outside of the fence for the past few weeks, appeared in the paddock again like Spring crocuses. Sheba rolling celebratorily on Annabel's new roof, Solomon getting so excited that when I was playing tag with him with Annabel's empty halter he seized the end of it in his mouth and ran away with it, as he sometimes did with string. I yelled in case the loop end of it caught on something and pulled out Solomon's teeth. Father Adams, blissfully en route from a mid-day session at the Rose and Crown, nearly dropped. God Almighty, he said, mopping his brow. He thought he was used to us by now. But when I shouted like that and a cat tore down the lane like a thunderbolt carrying a halter-now he'd seen everything, he said.

Not quite everything he hadn't. A few nights later I was sitting in the shed across the lane with Solomon. Guarding him against foxes, as a matter of fact. We never let them out unsupervised on winter evenings and when somebody roared for air or a desire to see the great outdoors one or other of us always went with them. This evening it was raining. Instead of walking up the lane Solomon and I were sitting in the open-fronted shed. I, to pass the ten minutes or so allocated to Fatso's airing, was shining my torch on the falling rain saying 'Look at the rain, Solomon'. At which moment Father Adams walked past, shone his torch on me and a Siamese sitting talking in the dark on a sand-heap, and demanded apprehensively 'Bist thee feelin' all right?'

Things having a habit of happening in threes, he strolled up the lane the following day and nearly stopped breathing altogether. The people in the modernised cottage had moved in some time before. One of their innovations had been a long, low lounge in stone with picture windows, built on at the side. Another had been a bridge over the stream to get their car across which Father Adams forecast would collapse at any moment – not for any structural reason but just because there hadn't been one there before – and kept going up to see if it had.

We always got the latest news when he came back. 'Plantin' their cabbages,' he would announce as he stumped past our gate. 'Seedin' their lawn.' 'Got their drains stopped up.' Always conveying an up-to-the-minute summary of what was going on, an implied disappointment that that was all that was happening and that the bridge hadn't fallen in yet, and the unfortunate impression, if we happened to have visitors, that he'd gone up there prospecting on our behalf.

'Thee's ought to see!' he greeted us stentoriously on this occasion from a good hundred yards away. We were wrong in gathering that the bridge had at last come up to expectations, however. What had happened was that autumn had come, the Segals had started their lounge fire on a free-standing, Swedish-style hearth that was plainly visible from the lane through their picture window, and had discovered that it smoked. Raising the hearth experimentally up and down on blocks they'd found that the correct height at which it didn't smoke was about three feet from the ground. Contemporarily correct inside their lounge, highly spectacular viewed from the lane when one saw a fire apparently burning on a shelf halfway up a wall – 'Thee's all be nuts!' was Father Adams' verdict when we explained that nowadays that was a perfectly normal idea.

A few days later I felt like agreeing with him as far as we were concerned. I called at the stables to thank Miss Linley, who'd been out with her riding school the morning we collected Annabel and Henry, and I hadn't seen her since. I told her about Henry's second escape and our returning him to his owner. Funny that Annabel didn't miss him, I said, since they got on so well together.

It was one of the biggest shocks in my career as a donkey-keeper when she said they certainly did – the morning after they'd run away they'd got married in her paddock. I felt myself turn pale. 'He's barren though, isn't he – like a mule?' she said in a hearty, used-to-animals voice which brought me partly back to consciousness. Of course he was, I agreed with her. Ha ha, of course he was. I was forgetting that.

It was Charles's turn to turn pale when I got home and told him. They were *supposed* to be barren, he groaned. One of the things the donkey-man had told him the day he brought Henry, though, which he'd forgotten to tell me but the man had said that in any case it was so remote it was bound to be all right, was that occasionally... there *had* been a couple of cases... where they weren't.

THIRTEEN

Working up for Winter

We kept quiet about the possibility of Annabel being *enceinte*. The Rector's wife would have worried. Miss Wellington would probably have bought pink wool and started knitting bootees. Father Adams – we could just see him going past the gate. Slapping at his knees. Guffawing 'When they're keen enough they're old enough' which was his usual ribald comment in a situation like this and spreading our discomfiture like wildfire round the Rose and Crown.

It quite possibly hadn't happened, of course – but a lot of little incidents seemed to fall into place after Miss Linley's revelation. The nose-nuzzling in the paddock. The elopement itself with Henry disappearing masterfully with his bride into the night. The scene next morning

– innocents that we were – when we saw them lying flat out in Miss Linley's field and thought they were tired from walking. Even when you came to think of it, said Charles darkly, the way we'd seen old Henry looking over the fence at the mare and foal and giving himself ideas.

So did Annabel's following after him the way she did the morning of their honeymoon and now not caring a button. And – or was it just the winter coming on – her increased fussiness about food.

She'd been easy enough to feed through the summer. Grass, water, bread, and a strong dislike for carrots. Apart from the cost – and a suspicion that we must have gone wrong somewhere because the whole point of donkeys, according to the article we'd read, was that even in winter all they needed was grazing, water, and a rough old hedge under which to shelter she'd been easy enough to feed in the autumn, too.

Hay, which disappeared into her stomach at the rate of nearly a bale a week now grass was short, and with which she contrived – by dint of emerging enquiringly from her house with a wisp of it in her mouth whenever we called her – to give an impression of being so hard at work we felt apologetic for having disturbed her. Oats, which as far as we could see she would have eaten by the sackful so we had to ration her to a saucepanful per meal, and Charles walking backwards through the paddock at feeding time, carrying a saucepan and warding off a donkey rearing joyfully after him on her hind legs like a Liberty horse, was matched on my part by the day she stopped in the lane, refused to come home until she had eaten all the ivy off a wall, and I fetched a saucepan of oats as bait. I started by waving it enticingly under her nose; I continued by jogging at an encouraging trot ahead of her down the lane; I ended things having got slightly out of hand – going flat out like a competitor in a pancake race, Annabel coming behind me like a greyhound, and I only just made it to the paddock.

Annabel liked oats so much that if we showed her an empty saucepan she would stick her head in it like a fencing mask and, while we held it in place over her nose, march hilariously round the field by way of demonstration. Annabel liked oats so much that when we decided we were still giving her too many and replaced her morning quota with bread she burrowed through it like a terrier, snorted with disgust when she found there were no oats underneath, and upset the bowl with her hoof. Annabel liked oats so much that when, a few weeks after Henry's departure, she suddenly went off them and took of all things to carrots, our eyebrows went up in alarm.

Full of Vitamins, she announced, chewing steadfastly away at the roots she'd previously hated. Made her feel Sick, she said, turning her head away when we offered her oats in our hands. Made her feel even Sicker, she insisted when we made her a hot bran mash, offered it to her knowing horses usually went mad about it, and after one wan sniff she turned languidly aside.

She could, she added as an afterthought – turning immediately back again to sniff the bag I had under my arm in case the mash was the wrong consistency – manage a little dry bran. So she took to bran and hot water consumed from separate bowls – as she often drank water through whatever she was eating the result was presumably mash anyway but Annabel preferred it like that – ate peppermints as avidly as ever, went capriciously off oven-dried bread for a week or two in favour of the same bread Soft with Honey On, and encouraged – as the next thing to worry us – rats.

We already, as we knew, had one rat. He lived in the cottage roof, disturbed us by coming in in the early hours and gnawing on the beam over our bedroom ceiling, and could be seen from time to time – which was the reason he'd taken up residence with us – slipping round the corner to eat the bread we put out for the birds in the yard. He was quite an establishment around the place and even Solomon and Sheba – he was, after all, a pretty big rat – didn't bother with him overmuch. Sometimes he had a session on the beam during the day whereupon the cats, snoozing comfortably on our bed, raised their heads, stared reproachfully at the ceiling, and went back to sleep. Sometimes Solomon did a routine look up a drainpipe like 'What The Butler Saw' and stuck his paw up it. Sometimes, if she had nothing else to do, Sheba sat in the guttering over the kitchen door. Overflowing it like a small blue broody hen, informing callers when they least expected it that she was Waiting up Here for the Rat – and he wished, said the postman, dropping our letters nervelessly into the mud one morning when she spoke to him in the very act of his handing them over, that we'd train our animals to be normal.

Once, after a particularly sleepless night ourselves, we caught the rat in a cage trap, carried it a mile into the hills with the coal tongs, set it free with a warning about disturbing people and started up another mystery. At five o'clock next morning somebody galloped belatedly across our bedroom ceiling, started gnawing post-haste at the beam, stopped when I hammered beneath it, and – after a minute or so's complete silence during which I got back into bed – dropped a stone like a bomb on the plaster-board. Whether our neighbour in the roof had found his way back and was mad with us, or whether it was a newly-imported girl-friend of his we'd captured and after a fruitless search for her he was mad at us about that we never knew. Only that it seemed to be the same rat we saw eating the bread in the yard next morning. Definitely that whoever it was was chewing away on the selfsame beam. And that we were practically walking somnambulists through lack of sleep and expecting the roof to cave in at any moment when suddenly, blessedly, he vanished.

He didn't vanish far. The next place we saw him – unmistakable from his size and light brown colouring –was up in Annabel's house, scuttling across the floor with a piece of bread in his mouth and making for a hole in the wall to which presumably he'd moved on the grounds that Annabel had a bigger stock of bread than the birds and nobody thumped on the ceiling at him in the night. And the next thing we knew he'd got friends up there.

Bread was disappearing from Annabel's bowl at breakfast time practically on a conveyor belt system. Annabel, a little belatedly, for it was her finickiness in leaving bread around that had started this business in the first place, was standing, while she ate, at Invasion Stations – behind her bowl and suspiciously facing the door, which was quite the wrong way round because the rats nipped out from behind her. Half the cats in the neighbourhood started sitting on the wall watching for the rats. Solomon kept going up and fighting the cats. Father Adams, listening to the howls that came constantly from behind Annabel's house where, from the sound of it, murder was being committed, said we couldn't even have rats could us, *peaceably* like other people.

We certainly couldn't. The howling was Solomon, with the other cats cornered in crevices or up trees, telling them what he'd do to them. Bite their ears off! he roared, undulating like an air-raid warning and probably deafening them for days. Pull their tails out! Punch their noses if they touched a twig on Siamese property! Which was all very well, but Solomon didn't catch the rats himself. All he did was come in with his eyes watering and frighten us into thinking he'd picked up a germ, until we realised it happened every time and the explanation was that the passion with which he'd been howling had made his eyes run. One day he also came in reeking of ammonia where a besieged adversary had sprayed at him in self-defence and we had, while he howled some more, to Dettol him. We were jolly glad when Annabel got keen on her food again, the rats and cats apparently disappeared, and life returned to normal.

As normal as it ever is, that is. We – it was now three weeks to Christmas – were having our sitting-room fireplace altered. The modern one, which had been the bugbear of our lives for years, taken out; an oak beam set in the wall as it must have been originally; and a simple, wide brick fireplace with an air-control principle behind it set back into the alcove.

Sidney, when we first asked him about doing the job, asked incredulously what did we want to move the old one out for. Nice shiny tiles, boiler and all behind, what did we want better than that? Sidney, reconciled eventually to our having a brick one, wilted again when we suggested setting it back in the alcove. Whip the first 'un out, he said persuasively; bung the brick 'un flat in its place – did we realise what it would mean in altering pipes alone if we went back into that wall? Sidney, bringing along his mate Norm to confirm the position when we still insisted on excavating the alcove, had a moment or two of intense hilarity when Norm said 'twould mean altering all the plumbing. I said we could do without hot water for a day or two. Norm and Sidney fell helpless on one another's shoulders at my innocence and said 'twould be more like a week but go ahead and order the thing if we wanted to. We did. The parts, ordered in September, arrived three months later. Sidney, when we told him, said Lumme he thought we'd forgotten that lot, he was in the middle of decorating his bathroom. Pressed for co-operation on account of the nearness of Christmas he said Norm and his other mate Ern might possibly help him. And so the job was done.

At weekends and evenings. Taking just over a fortnight and seeming like all eternity. With the windows open to the winter blasts to get the rubble out – half a lorry load at least said Sidney and Co., gleefully tipping it with Charles' co-operation into the storm ditch outside the gate and I knew, come January, we'd have to dig it out again. Discovering three flues built one behind the other in the chimney wall, the bar on which the first cottager's wife must have hung her cauldrons, but – to the team's great disappointment – no hidden gold.

The great oak beam was sawn to size on the sitting-room floor and hoisted into place, Sidney commenting relievedly that he was glad that was in. He wouldn't, he said (which was the first we'd heard of it) have slept in the place the last couple of nights himself, he wouldn't, with a hole like that in the wall and nothing to hold it up. The plumbing was disconnected and, through somebody not turning a screw tightly enough, water flooded the floor amid the sawdust and cement. A hole was made for the new air control pipe through from the sitting-room to the conservatory – a hole which went down like a mine and under and up, and as soon as the team went home the cats started going down like a mine and under and up too, yelling their surprise at finding themselves among the chrysanthemums and nipping round to the back door to be let in and try some more.

When the hole was filled in again Solomon took to being the Third Man in the Vienna sewers – creeping mysteriously around under dust covers and narrowly escaping being sat on. Sheba sat dramatically on the carpet, which was piled on the table with the underfelt and the table pushed against a window. The curtains were down on account of the dust and Sheba, perched perpetually on her mound of carpet, not only attracted far more attention from passers-by than our activities would otherwise have had, but at night, when the lights (without shades) were on, she added a waif-like touch to the scene that made it look as if we were either in for a Christmas like the Cratchits or else, as Charles remarked, as if she was expecting the floods at any minute and was already on Mount Ararat.

I was sweating pretty hard about Christmas myself, but we made it all right. The fireplace went in. The mess was cleared up. Ern, working dementedly in a clockwise direction, painted the entire room with two coats of white with the biggest brush he could find while Sidney and Norm put the finishing touches to the mantelpiece.

Not, even then, that the job was without its involvements. Sidney arrived one night towards the end of the period, tired out as were we all with the effort it had entailed, and informed us that his cousin Bert had called the night before about his staircase. Sidney, it seemed, had some time previously promised Bert that one of these days he'd alter it for him – to one of these modern styles, said Sidney, with open treads and bamboo poles to grow ivy up.

Fraught, apparently, with the same desire to have ivy and bamboo poles on their stairs for Christmas as we had to sit by an old-style fireplace, Bert and his wife had spent the previous Sunday stripping the staircase; come joyfully round to tell Sidney they were ready for him to start work; Sidney, exhausted with our little lot, said not before Christmas he wasn't; and when Bert's wife said but what were they going to do, they'd taken all the paper off, Sidney (a remark which we gathered he now regretted) had suggested they stick it back on again.

This has more to do with the story of Annabel than it may seem. While Sidney and Co. worked in their spare time on our fireplace, you see, they discussed these other jobs with us. At the beginning of the period they were working during the day on a farmhouse in the neighbourhood whose owners were restoring it to its original Elizabethan state, and Sidney's condition of near apoplexy at having to take up a fine polished parquet floor in the hall and replace it with flagstones (guess what he'd been doing all day, he said resignedly on one occasion; going round the outhouses, tapping the floor for flagstones, digging 'em up as if they was gold and washing 'em) was equalled only by his indignation the following night when he said what did we think he was doing now? Taking up the kitchen floor on account of its consisting of cracked old flagstones which they hadn't been able to find enough of in the outhouses. Transporting it by wheelbarrow through to the hall – the place, said Sidney, was nothing but duckboards and the cook was going mad. Replacing it in the kitchen, he informed us in a voice full of tragedy, not even by the parquet but by blooming old red cement.

By the time the fireplace was finished Sidney and Co. were engaged on another curious task. Digging up the village maypole, which was normally a permanent fixture in the school playground, and erecting it in the local guest house which had borrowed it for the Christmas festivities. Not to ask *him* why they were doing maypole dances at Christmas, said Sidney exasperatedly. For the same reason people took up flagstones in their kitchen and bunged 'em down in their hall he expected. What got him was that they had to keep putting it up and down. Up in the morning for the kids to practise, down at night for the guest house visitors to play table tennis. He and his mates was marching up and down the road like a picket patrol, he said, and if it came down when they was gigglegacking round it at Christmas and hit 'em on their silly gert heads 'twould serve 'em right.

Sidney told us about the maypole. Sidney, on his visits to raise or lower the maypole at the guest house, told Mrs. Reynolds about us and Annabel...

It was the fault of the season, of course. People singing Little Donkey on the radio. Miss Wellington coming by while we were giving Annabel supper in her house saying what a picture she made by lantern-light. The Rector recalling the year the choirboys, in scarlet cassocks and ruffs, toured the village singing carols with lanterns slung on poles. Coming over the hill in procession like a mediaeval picture, he said. Singing so sweetly it brought the tears to one's eyes. The only year they'd done it, alas, for most of them caught colds...

When after that Mrs. Reynolds rang us to say could she – with memories of Dolly and Desmond – have Annabel in her Christmas entertainment, what could we say but yes.

FOURTEEN

A Quiet Country Christmas

What could we say but yes, either, when the carol party got wind of Mrs. Reynolds' venture and asked if Annabel could accompany them as well. To brighten things up, they said, as the carol party, since the year the choir caught cold, was now a sober, adult affair with everybody in headscarves and gum-boots. The only concession to a Dickensian atmosphere was the lantern borrowed from the choir and borne aloft on its pole by Mr Smithson – and that, said the carol party organiser resignedly, couldn't look very romantic, could it, when one opened one's front door and saw him holding it in a homburg and woollen gloves.

So Annabel went carol-singing, wearing a yellow wool scarf with bobbles to add colour to the occasion, padding virtuously along the lanes beneath the lantern, insisting on being first up people's paths and occasionally getting jammed in gateways with Mr Smithson, who was also used to being first in with his pole.

There were minor difficulties, as there always are on such occasions. Annabel going the wrong side of telegraph poles on her lead, for instance, and continually bringing the party to a kaleidoscopic halt. And the incident at the Duggans' bungalow, blocked by what in the flickering lantern-light appeared to be Mr Duggan having suddenly gone mad and erected Glastonbury Tor across his drive. We nearly dropped when the lights went on and it turned out to be ten tons of manure ordered by Mr Duggan for his garden and delivered in his absence by a man who, with nobody around to stop him had deposited it with alacrity on the doorstep and departed. We pulled ourselves together. We sang Noel on one side of the manure heap. The Duggans joined in invisibly on the other a trifle dispiritedly, perhaps, at the prospect of having to get up next day and shovel it all away, but the tradition of singing in one's porch with the carollers has to be kept up. And Annabel Aaaw-Hoooed at the end to let them know she was with us and got a mince pie over the top. Annabel's personal tradition about carol-singing, this; she'd already achieved six since starting out.

Wonderful how people rose to the occasion in the country, wasn't it? enthused a three-months-out-from-town member of the party as we plodded up the hill. Hardly were the words out of his mouth than a situation arose to which it was practically impossible to rise, however, and Annabel stopped. Faced with what she recognised as a long dark trek across to the other part of the village, whereas behind her was a lane of houses with mince pies in, she said she'd done enough carol-singing for the night. She was going back the way she came. Possibly visiting friends on the Way, she insisted, pulling back so stubbornly on her haunches it was like trying to move the Rock of Gibraltar.

Charles and I pulled. Some of the others pushed. Mr Smithson stood self-consciously by with the lantern. A wit passing by to the Rose and Crown remarked on the resemblance to Uncle Tom Cobleigh and asked which fair we were going to this time.

We made it in the end with the aid of peppermints donated by the pub. Annabel completed her rounds smelling alternately of peppermint and mince pies; looked angelic in her scarf when people came to their doors and petted her; walked alongside us – except for her lapse on the hilltop and the occasional sorties round telegraph poles – as if she was one of the gang; looked suitably modest when at the end the organiser counted up the takings and said it was more, thanks to our dear little donkey, than ever before.

Annabel, said Charles as we ambled glowingly back down to the cottage with her, was wonderful. One could do anything with that donkey. He'd been thinking while he was singing, he said, and he knew what we could do with her for Mrs Reynolds' entertainment. He'd go as an Arab in a burnous.

You could have knocked me down with a manure heap. Mrs Reynolds wasn't doing a Christmas play. She was this year – hence the maypole – doing Ye Olde Englishe Village. In, presumably, Springtime. Admittedly no specific part had been laid on for Annabel other than to generally charm the audience, but we might, I thought, have found something more in keeping with the general theme than Charles in a burnous.

Charles, alas, with his predilection for unusual headgear, fancied a burnous. He'd look much more appropriate with a donkey as an Arab, he said, than a farmhand with a smock and hayfork. He also, as I knew full well, had once had his photograph taken in a burnous in the Middle East and rather fancied himself as Lawrence of Arabia. So he got busy with a couple of sheets and one of those thick woollen cords with tassels used for looping back old-fashioned curtains which he borrowed from Mrs Adams; frightened Sheba out of her wits by coming down the stairs in it just when she was going up to see what he was doing; pronounced himself all set for the fray...

The entertainment was planned for Boxing Day. It might have been all right even then had Charles been able to do what he intended and practise with Annabel on Boxing Morning. On Christmas night, however, Solomon disorganised the house completely with a bilious attack.

It began with the cats – Charles' Aunt Ethel being in temporary possession of the spare room – being put to bed, complete with earth-boxes, in the sitting-room. It continued with Solomon deciding to use his earth-box before he went to sleep – magnificent he looked, too, posed majestically in his yellow plastic bowl on a plum-coloured carpet behind a turquoise door – and discovering that he couldn't. Sick! he howled, panicking immediately as Solomon always does. Call the Vet! Fetch the Doctor! Tum Wouldn't Work, he explained woefully as we came running to see what was wrong.

Nobody but Solomon would get his stomach stuck on Christmas night. Nobody but Solomon, either, would have eaten so much all day – turkey, cream and caramel blancmange in a practically non-stop round since lunchtime – that the effort of trying to use his box made him sick. He kept getting into his box, howling about his stomach, getting out again, being sick. Long after we'd put the lights out and crept quietly to bed in the hope that he might stop worrying in the darkness and go to bed himself, we could still hear him complaining down below.

We came down to him three times in the night. We were up again at dawn. His stomach, he informed us, still wouldn't work. He'd been sick six times on the carpet. A fine Christmas night this had been, we said wearily, sitting there waiting for daylight and the time to call the Vet.

Actually Solomon resolved the problem himself. As daylight grew and presumably he imagined Aunt Ethel would be awake he went upstairs, scratched tearfully at the spare room door and demanded to be let in. Wanted to use his Box, he shouted when she asked who was there. In his Corner where he was Used to it, he insisted, flatly refusing to consider it when we put it placatingly on the landing.

It was a good thing she was one of the family. What anyone else would have said – to be turned out of bed at daybreak on Boxing Morning while we marched in with an earth-box and Solomon seated himself with a reproachful wail that it was all her fault and how'd she like it if somebody slept in her bathroom when she wanted to use it – I cannot think. As it was, we all went down for a cup of tea, ten minutes later there was a howl at which we leapt for the hall thinking that at the very least Solomon had turned himself inside out – and there he was coming down the stairs. All Right Now, he advised us, with a lighthearted spring at Sheba by way of celebration. Anybody for Breakfast? he roared, taking up position by the refrigerator.

Which was all very well, but after that we were exhausted. We lay in chairs most of the morning recovering our nerves. By the time the van came to take Annabel and us to the entertainment Charles hadn't done any practising at all at being an Arab and we were still half asleep on our feet. Which was how Charles came to be kicked.

I held our little donkey at the guest house while Charles put on his costume. Annabel, when Charles strode billowingly from the changing room looking like the Red Shadow, got the wind up and said – too late I remembered she didn't like white things – that he was a Ghost. Charles said Come on, Annabel, not to be silly. Annabel said she wasn't silly, he was a Ghost and she was going to kick him. Charles, half asleep and incommoded by the trailing sheets, didn't jump fast enough. And when she caught him on the shinbone he yelled louder than Solomon.

We let her go after that. She roamed amiably around the room among the guests. Ate enough tea for six. Stood winsomely at the foot of the maypole with mistletoe behind her ears while the children danced around it and everybody sighed and wished for cameras. Wonderfully tame, our little donkey, said a visitor, coming over to where, with Charles still soulfully rubbing his shin, we waited by the sideline. He expected we were fond of her. What, he enquired, gazing interestedly at Charles's get-up, was he supposed to be? A Druid?

Our major Christmas adventure was yet to come, however. Two nights later, with a mist lying low over the valley and the trees dripping wetly in the darkness, we woke around four o'clock in the morning to hear a car outside our gate. It stopped, waited for a while, turned and went back up again. An unusual occurrence at that hour in our isolated part of the world, and doubly so when half an hour later what was apparently the same car drove at top speed down the hill, passed the cottage, and jolted on up the lane. When a few minutes later there was a thud as the car went into the ditch, followed immediately by a frantic whirring of the back wheels as somebody tried to get it out again, we were even more perturbed.

I, quite frankly, was scared practically rigid. Charles was for going up to see what it was – armed, he assured me, with a tyre lever – but I wasn't having any. Supposing it was a desperado, I said. Somebody having committed a bank robbery, for instance. Trying to get away into the hills, for nobody would go rattling up an isolated track at four in the morning for any normal reason. The man wasn't injured otherwise he wouldn't be trying to get the car out. On the other hand, why was he trying so frantically to get it out himself instead of coming to ask for help? I, I said determinedly, was going to call the police.

It is surprising how clearly one's mind works in an emergency. Like a member of MI5 I felt, creeping down the stairs in the darkness (better not to show a light); sitting with the telephone on the hall floor (sometimes they shoot at one through windows); dialling 999. That was a bit difficult because I couldn't, what with the darkness and my trembling like an aspen, remember which end of the dial the 9 was, but I got it in the end. Whispered my message into the mouthpiece and received instructions not to go out of doors on any account; they'd be with us as soon as possible...

The driver was still reversing hysterically when I went back to the window. It was a nerve-racking business, keeping watch through the swirling mist. I jumped like a grasshopper when there was a scuffling sound from the spare room but it was only the cats, disturbed by the noise, getting up to look out of their window. My heart nearly stopped entirely when a second or two later Annabel, whom I'd quite forgotten, let out a mighty blast complaining that she, too, had been disturbed. It frightened me, used to her as I was. What it did to the driver goodness knew, except after that there was no more revving.

When the police car arrived, sweeping silently down the hill with its roof-light flashing, there was no man either. Only a car tilted into the ditch; our assurance that the driver hadn't come back past the cottage; and a report from a second patrol car which arrived a short while later that there was no sign of him around the village.

We gathered, from snatches of conversation, that they knew who they were looking for. We gathered so even more when we got up next morning and there outside the cottage were three police cars, an Inspector and two Sergeants conferring over a map, a couple of men with walkie-talkie outfits and a handler with a tracker dog.

Excitement followed excitement. Footprints were found under a tree up the lane and, while the police slapped chagrinedly at their helmets, turned out to be ours, where we'd taken the cats for a walk the previous evening. The cats, unable to go out on account of the dog, sat rubbernecking at him from the hall window with ears stuck up like radar aerials. Annabel paraded importantly back and forth along her fence – ten paces, right wheel; ten paces, left wheel – till a constable said she looked like a top-cop on patrol duty. Half the village gathered outside our gate, including Miss Wellington who pushed worriedly through the crowd to ask the Inspector who was missing, was it Annabel?

We weren't a bit surprised when we heard on the one o'clock news that some men were missing from a local prison. It was a bit of an anti-climax, however, when it transpired that our man wasn't one of them. That someone in the village had given a party. The first car we'd heard, at four in the morning, was bringing home a girl who'd helped at the party. The second car, a short while later, had contained a guest from town who, mistaking his way in the fog, had landed in our lane instead of on the main road. He'd tried – probably being a little merrier than he should have been – to get the car out of the ditch himself and had failed. He'd been frightened clean out of his wits when Annabel brayed at him, had gone haring back by a track through the woods to his friend's house and then, feeling a little braver by that time and not liking on second thoughts to disturb him, had found a nearby barn and slept it off till lunchtime.

Might have been a criminal though, said Father Adams sagely. Nice to know we knew our onions and the police were so quick off the mark. It was indeed. Except that Charles, after that, got the idea of keeping a tyre-lever permanently under the bedroom carpet in case we ever needed to know our onions again.

There, he assured me, it was invisible but handy. There it clonked hollowly under my feet every time I made the bed. And there, going up to repair a floorboard and me not remembering to remove it first, Sidney incredulously discovered it one morning and a fresh bit of news went round the village. That we kept tyre levers for burglar protection under our carpets.

FIFTEEN

To Be or Not to Be

One might have expected life to be a little humdrum after that, but we had our diversions. A tile blowing off the roof in a gale, for instance, and Charles going up in the dark to replace it and coming resignedly down with the cause. A marsh tit's nest. Built under the roof in the previous spring. Swollen with winter rain, which was why it had pushed up the tiles. Made, Charles pointed out, of donkey hair, and he bet we were the only people in England who adopted a donkey and got their tiles blown off as a result.

Then the stream – which normally disappears down a swallet-hole up the lane – rose as it always does in the January rains, ran down to us, couldn't get through our ditch on account of the rubble from the fireplace, and no doubt we were the only people in England doing that. Digging the darned stuff out again. With the stream gushing down the middle of the road. The cats sitting happily on the coalhouse roof advising everybody who passed that we were digging it out fast before the policeman saw us. Annabel informing the world from up the lane that she didn't do it and could she please be moved to a place of safety. And Timothy, engaged to help us in return for cash towards a racing bike, leaving us goggle-eyed with his account of every day getting his jean-legs shrunk in the stream, every night hanging them up to dry over his mother's Aga with the legs tied at the ends with string and filled with stones – and every morning, our helper assured us with aplomb, the jeans as good as new again and the legs stretched back to normal.

We had a morning when we sat up in bed to find a heron on our garden path. Following the stream, no doubt; coming down to land when he spotted the outline of our fish pool; flapping off as cross as a crow when he found that Charles hadn't finished it yet and there were still no goldfish in it. We had a morning when we sat up in bed to find a squirrel on the lawn. Digging under an apple tree, coming up triumphantly with a brace of our biggest cobnuts and we'd wondered where they'd got to in the previous autumn. We had also, recurring like an echo through the tempo of our activities, the question of whether Annabel was to be a mother.

If faddiness was anything to go by she was probably having triplets. She still ate bran in preference to oats. She rejected two entire bales of hay on the grounds that she didn't like that kind and we had to get some more. She announced that she wanted her drinking water hot. A decision understandable in January, when we'd heated the water to prevent it freezing, but slightly suspicious come April, when the sun shone, the cats sunbathed on her shelter roof and Annabel, confronted by a pail of fresh cold water, pouted her lips at it and said she still required it Hot.

What with that, a liking for carrots and a sudden passion for orange peel – she found some on the hill one day, savoured it as if it were caviare, and thereafter a customs inspector had nothing on Annabel going through the waste-basket at the bus-stop every time she passed – things looked pretty black indeed.

There was no point in consulting the Vet. That became obvious as Spring rolled on and practically every day we opened the papers to read of unexpected foals.

A twenty-year old donkey whose owner said he couldn't think how she'd managed it had had a little blackjack. A small bay mare, bought for a greengrocer's round by a man with a lifetime's experience of horses, had scared the daylights out of him by lying down in the shafts on her first trip out with the cauliflowers and producing a small bay filly. A little girl's riding pony, whose owner could only inform reporters that recently Polly hadn't seemed keen on going to pony-club meetings though previously she'd *liked* the other ponies, had had a white one with spots... The papers quoted veterinary experts as saying you often couldn't tell with horses.

We certainly couldn't tell with Annabel. One minute we thought she was and prescribed plenty of greens for vitamins. Her own paddock being threadbare after the winter's eating we tethered her up on the hill to get them, trekked leisurely back to the cottage – and within minutes were running back up again like mad. Annabel, by way of amusement and presumably trying to snap her tether at the same time, was up there galloping furiously down the slope like the Charge of the Light Brigade, pulling taut on the end of her rope with a jerk that must be knocking the triplets for six if she had them, plodding steadfastly back to the starting point like a skier returning up a ski-run, and doing it over again.

Later we decided she couldn't possibly be in foal, the trouble was she was eating too much and we ought to cut her rations down. The result of that was that Annabel's stomach, which despite her non-stop eating habits had rumbled at intervals ever since we'd known her like a distant train on the Underground, now began to rumble more loudly, like an incipiently active volcano. The day we gave her a reduced allowance of hay, stayed to clean out her house, heard what we thought was Timothy trundling his go-cart down the lane and looked up to discover that it wasn't Timothy at all but Annabel's stomach rumbling, we gave up putting her on a diet. We decided to let nature take its course, fed her so that her stomach remained muted though steadfastly barrel-shaped, and waited. For what looked like being rather a long wait, seeing that it takes a horse eleven months to foal; presumably (though we couldn't find it even in Britannica) it takes a donkey the same; and it would be October before we knew.

Meanwhile, so that we wouldn't get ennuied while we waited, the bird-mating season set in at the cottage. Missel thrushes nested trustingly in the damson tree, we showed them by way of a treat to Miss Wellington, and created a ripe old situation there. We had Miss Wellington hovering constantly by our gate in case when the young were hatched they fell out on to our path. Miss Wellington nipping smartly across to the hedge to pick dandelions when anybody passed – 'To make wine,' she informed passers-by; 'To put them off the scent,' she advised us; with the result that after being put off the scent daily for a week Father Adams enquired interestedly of us what th'old girl was making as much wine as that for; planning a Batchanalia? When the birds hatched they did start falling out, too, and, as nutty as Miss Wellington, we put straw down for them to fall on and kept going out when she wasn't around to return them to the nest.

How they escaped the cats was a miracle, said Miss Wellington. Actually it was because the mouse-hunting season had started also and our March of the Siamese Cats was returning, not, as it often did, via the front gate with an excursion up the damson tree for exercise, but in a crow's flight line from the paddock. Over the wall, down the path, up the stairs to our bedroom where they usually stored their catches and where one day, to our horror, we found they had stored a rat. Only a young one, stone-cold dead on its back, but where there was one there were others.

There were, when we started to look for them, dozens. Multiplying like flies, no doubt, with the warmer weather; attracted by Annabel's bread; and coming not only from the walls of her house but trekking, at feeding time, down the valley. Like a portage procession through the Khyber Pass, said Charles, who watched astounded one morning from across on the hillside as they filed familiarly down a track from some ruins in a neighbouring field, disappeared into

Annabel's house, and a second or two later filed familiarly back up again carrying whacking great lumps of bread.

Something had to be done, of course. We couldn't leave the cats to deal with them – otherwise, as we knew full well, one day they'd come up against a big one and somebody would be bitten. We couldn't trap them on account of the danger to the birds and cats. We couldn't call in the Pest Officer and have them poisoned for the same reason. On the other hand, for our own sakes and everybody else's, we couldn't have them multiplying like this. So Charles, with the cats shut in the cottage, Annabel on the lawn and a bowl of bread in her house for bait, shot them. Not before we'd noticed something interesting, however. On the whole the rats made Annabel nervous. She stamped her feet at them; kicked when she was eating and they rustled in the straw; looked worried from time to time at their entrance holes in the corners. Not, however, when it came to a certain light-brown rat. A rat whom we, too, recognised.

He could come out of his hole with impunity. One night, when we went up to see Annabel at dusk, we discovered him actually feeding with her at her bowl. We watched amazed from the paddock as he stood up on his hind legs, leaned into her bowl and ate nose to nose with our donkey. We watched even more amazed when, as the level of bran went down, the rat got into the bowl, Annabel went on eating, and when he got in her way she just tossed him out with her nose. Even then, while we stood there pop-eyed with incredulity, the rat unperturbedly climbed back again.

We didn't shoot him. He was a rat of character. If we kept the rest of them down, we decided, he could hardly propagate the valley on his own. So Charles despatched the rest. The fawn one was allowed to go free. In order not to encourage a further invasion we fed Annabel, as it was now full Spring, in the open field where rats hesitate to go...

Meanwhile Annabel had a further adventure. We were having lunch one day when the owner of Misha the Alsatian arrived with a distracted expression on her face and asked whether she could borrow Annabel for a while.

She had, she explained, a two-year-old called Monarch, destined to become a racehorse. Her other horses had gone away to grass. Monarch, kept behind because he needed building up as thoroughbreds sometimes do, was pining for the others and refusing his food. She wondered if Annabel could help him eat.

Annabel, we assured her, could help anybody eat. Probably only by getting the idea from watching her that if they didn't hurry up there'd be a famine. But they'd eat. She even made us feel ravenous at times. Which was why, that evening, the village saw another local procession. Our taking Annabel over to meet Monarch.

Some of them, since Monarch lived quite near the centre of the village, saw the moment when they actually did meet when Monarch towered over his gate to sniff at her and Annabel, with one look at the tallest horse she had ever seen, put her tail between her legs and started determinedly for home.

Still more of them witnessed the next scene. When we led Annabel into the field, she hid behind us, Monarch tried to get round us to look at her, and the lot of us – since as fast as we sidestepped evasively so did Annabel behind us and so did Monarch in front – did a veleta across the field.

Roused, no doubt, by banging on one another's doors, a crowd that would have done credit to a town crier witnessed the scene when we ran to encourage Annabel, Monarch ran too to catch us up, and, encircled with animals like an Indian attack, we went flat out for our lives.

Eventually we left them together, however. Eventually they touched noses and made friends. Magically, with Annabel feeding beside him and he looking proudly down at her, Monarch started to graze. She could sleep soundly tonight now, said Mrs Jennings, as we slipped off up the lane.

Not perhaps so soundly as she hoped. Somebody passing our cottage later that evening reported Monarch and Annabel going round their paddock like the Valkyries. Somebody else, passing our way at closing time, reported Mrs Jennings and her husband going like Valkyries too. Trying to catch them, they said – for one of the conditions we'd made about lending Annabel was that she should be locked in for safety at night. They'd caught them. Led them in. Annabel first, reported the onlooker; Monarch refused to move a step till he'd seen Annabel put into a loose box ahead of him. Let them out the next morning, continued the report, when Annabel was seen heading through the vegetable garden as her personal short cut to the paddock and Monarch gallivanting after her.

Gallivanting was the word. The whole of that day, apparently, he never stopped chasing Annabel. Whether – which was something we hadn't given thought to – it was because she was a girl. In which case, said Charles, her marriage to Henry was no doubt null and void but in the course of time we could expect a donkey foal with legs like a racehorse. Whether, which was the Jennings' interpretation, she was just too small for Monarch... From the point of view of *playing*, explained Mrs. Jennings – with those little legs and that long coat and Monarch chasing her round like a puppy.

But that night they brought her back again. Monarch was eating like a horse, they said, thanks to her. To keep up the good work they'd borrowed a companion for him more his own size and now he was chasing that one round the field...

Never, in all the time we'd had her, had we seen a more thoughtful donkey than the one who walked into her house that night, looked appreciatively at her bed, and snorted with contentment as we put her hurdle up. East, West, Home Was Best, said Annabel as she lay down in the straw. She didn't like racehorses, she said as we crept quietly away with the cats.

Postscript

So there, for the moment, we are. The one thing we have learned from our year of donkey keeping is that donkeys don't eat nettles. Not straight from the field, anyway. Only when they are cut down and wilted so the sting doesn't hurt their mouths, said an expert who told us about it one day. And wasn't that reasonable, when one came to consider it?

Perfectly. Except that Annabel – put at last among the fruit trees, with the bracken removed, cages round the apples (better, we thought, than a cage around Annabel), the nettles cut and wilted and nothing to do but pick them up – didn't eat the nettles. She ate all the raspberry canes. Prickles and all, announced Charles, arriving starkly with the news that she'd mown them all to the ground. And then we moved her to another patch of ground and she ate our cultivated hollies. Prickles and all too, until all that remained of months of cherishing by Charles were two little main-stems with the labels fluttering like distress signals from their tops. Got mixed up with the Dandelions, was Annabel's explanation.

That is why, when she is out of her paddock now, she usually has Charles in attendance. Keeping an eye on her while he works to prevent further misunderstandings about dandelions. Unless, of course, she is on the lawn under my jurisdiction. Chasing Solomon and Sheba, who play Donkeys and Indians with her willingly for the perturbation of passers-by. Greeting the tradesmen, who grow nimbler day by day at nipping backwards through the gate with Annabel's nose in their baskets. Clattering into the kitchen for refreshment, which has led to a further discovery. That Annabel likes liquor.

She likes, at any rate, the top off fermenting barley wine. Nectar, commented Annabel when I experimentally offered her the skimmings. Nourishing, she announced, practically knocking the table over in her anxiety to have some more. It took two of us to get her back to the paddock that night, and she ate my tape-measure as she went.

We have very peculiar cats. We now have a peculiar donkey.

Any bets, asks Charles, that come October we have another peculiar member of the household? About two feet high with a liking for barley wine? With ears and a voice like Annabel?

CATS
IN THE BELFRY

'The most enchanting cat book ever'
Jilly Cooper

DOREEN TOVEY

CATS IN THE BELFRY

Doreen Tovey

£6.99   Paperback   ISBN: 978 1 84024 452 6

'It wasn't, we discovered as the months went by, that Sugieh was particularly wicked. It was just that she was a Siamese.'

Animal lover Doreen and her husband Charles acquire their first Siamese kitten to rid themselves of an invasion of mice. But Sugieh is not just any cat. She's an actress, a prima donna, an iron hand in a delicate, blue-pointed glove. She quickly establishes herself as queen of the house, causing chaos daily by screaming like a banshee, chewing up telegrams, and tearing holes in anything made of wool.

First published over forty years ago, this warm and witty classic tale is a truly enjoyable read for anyone who's ever been owned by a cat.

'If there is a funnier book about cats I for one do not want to read it. I would hurt myself laughing, might even die of laughter'
THE SCOTSMAN

'Every so often, there comes along a book – or if you're lucky books – which gladden the heart, cheer the soul... Just such books are those written by Doreen Tovey'   CAT WORLD

'A chaotic, hilarious and heart-wrenching love affair with this most characterful of feline breeds'   THE PEOPLE'S FRIEND

CATS
IN MAY

From the bestselling author of
Cats In The Belfry

DOREEN TOVEY

CATS IN MAY

Doreen Tovey

£6.99   Paperback   ISBN: 978 1 84024 497 7

'All our animals showed their independence at a dishearteningly early age.'

The Toveys attempt to settle down to a quiet life in the country. Unfortunately for them, however, their tyrannical Siamese cats have other ideas.

From causing an uproar on the BBC to staying out all night and claiming to have been kidnapped, Sheba and Solomon's outrageous behaviour leaves the Toveys at their wits' end. Meanwhile Doreen has to contend with her husband's disastrous skills as a handyman, and a runaway tortoise called Tarzan.

Both human and animal characters come to life on the page, including Sidney the problem-prone gardener and Blondin the brandy-swilling squirrel. This witty and stylish tale will have animal-lovers giggling to the very last page.

'No-one writes about cats with more wit, humour and affection than Doreen Tovey. Every word is a delight!'

THE PEOPLE'S FRIEND

THE
NEW BOY

From the bestselling author of Cats In The Belfry

DOREEN TOVEY

THE NEW BOY

Doreen Tovey

£6.99   Paperback   ISBN: 978 1 84024 517 2

'So there we were, driving along with an earth-box, a bag of turkey and, squalling his head off on my knee in Sheba's basket, the new boy.'

The Toveys are no strangers to disaster, particularly the Siamese-related kind, but when their beloved Solomon dies unexpectedly, they're faced with a completely new type of problem – do they find another cat to replace the one they've lost?

The animals always win in the Tovey household and this time is no exception. It is with the interests of Solomon's (very audibly) grieving sister Sheba at heart that Doreen and Charles set off in search of Solomon Secundus, affectionately known as Seeley.

Joined by a myriad of endearing characters, Seeley ensures he's living up to Solomon's standards in just the amount of time it takes to fall in a fishpond. This is an enchanting tale that will tickle your funny bone and tug on your heartstrings all in the same breath.

www.summersdale.com